South-Western

WORDPERFECT® 6.0 FOR WINDOWS™

QUICK COURSE

Kathleen P. Wagoner
PROFESSOR EMERITA
BALL STATE UNIVERSITY
MUNCIE, IN

Neil J. Wagoner
WAGONER & ASSOCIATES
MUNCIE, IN

SOUTH-WESTERN EDUCATIONAL PUBLISHING

Copyright © 1995
by SOUTH-WESTERN EDUCATIONAL PUBLISHING
Cincinnati, Ohio

ALL RIGHTS RESERVED

The text of this publication, or any part thereof, may not be reproduced or transmitted in any form or by any means, electronic or mechanical, including photocopying, recording, storage in an information retrieval system, or otherwise, without the prior written permission of the publisher.

I(T)P
International Thomson Publishing

South-Western Educational Publishing is a division of International Thomson Publishing Inc. The ITP trademark is used under license.

ISBN: 0-538-64061-8

1 2 3 4 5 6 7 8 H 00 99 98 97 96 95 94

Printed in the United States of America

Marketing Manager:	Brad Van Alfen
Acquisitions Editor:	Janie Schwark
Production Manager:	Anne Noschang
Sr. Production Editor:	Alan Biondi
Production Editor:	Carol Spencer
Sr. Designer:	Nicky Jones
Production Artist:	Sophia Renieris
Cover Photographer:	Marjory Dressler

WordPerfect is a registered trademark of WordPerfect Corporation.

Preface

WordPerfect 6.0 for Windows: Quick Course is designed as a self-paced instructional guide to be used either by individuals working alone or in a classroom setting. The vocabulary of the text is appropriate for high school, post-secondary, or adult learners.

MESSAGE TO THE LEARNER

Welcome to WordPerfect 6.0 for Windows. You will find that WordPerfect 6.0 for Windows takes advantage of the graphic nature of the Windows interface. You will see how your document looks and, as you edit it, most changes you make will be instantly visible. With the Power Bar, Button Bar, templates, and macros available to you, you will find that WordPerfect offers a range of powerful text creation, manipulation, and editing features that help to simplify and speed up document preparation.

This book is based on the assumption that you already know how to use your computer and you have some familiarity with word processing concepts, as well as the basics of the Windows interface.

This book also assumes that the WordPerfect 6.0 for Windows program has been installed and that you are familiar with the basic ways of interacting with Windows. In addition, this book assumes that your computer has been set up to use the Common User Access (CUA) keyboard and that you have not changed any default settings using the Preferences command.

The lessons are designed to be performed in sequence; in many cases, features and exercises build upon those learned in previous lessons. Exercise documents are used a number of times throughout the lessons to eliminate the need for extra keying.

Follow directions carefully to become familiar with and to understand the power of WordPerfect 6.0 for Windows.

LESSON FEATURES

Each lesson contains the following:

- Learning Objectives to preview a lesson's contents
- Explanations of WordPerfect 6.0 for Windows features and when to use them
- Step-by-step instructions to use the features
- Hands-on exercises to apply and reinforce learning
- Questions for Review to reinforce student learning

In addition, there are:
- Questions to provide students with an understanding of the documentation provided by WordPerfect
- Questions to provide students with practice in troubleshooting with Reveal Codes
- Review Exercises placed strategically to apply and reinforce previous learning
- Culminating Project to apply many of the features learned throughout the text

A UNIQUE FEATURE

This book gives special emphasis to how to troubleshoot with Reveal Codes. Many of the lessons following the presentation of the Reveal Codes feature provide a special problem for using Reveal Codes.

STUDENT HELPS

A Study Guide listing lesson titles with space to check off completed work is provided.

The Appendices provide additional information about customizing the Button Bar, Power Bar, Menu Bar, and Status Bar, as well as Troubleshooting with Reveal Codes.

Also available is a template disk containing many of the documents in the hands-on exercises. Although the keying of the exercises enhances learning, for those whose time is limited, the use of the prerecorded documents can enable them to complete this text more quickly.

MANUAL

The teacher's manual contains the following:
- Teaching suggestions for each lesson
- A suggested time schedule
- A list of documents on the template disk
- Solutions for Questions for Review, Reference Questions, and Troubleshooting with Reveal Codes problems
- Solutions for hands-on and Review exercises
- Three production tests with solutions
- One concepts test with solutions

ACKNOWLEDGMENTS

We would like to give our special thanks to our husband and father, W. J. Wagoner, for his constant support. Thanks also to George A. Wagoner for his excellent contributions and to Janie Schwark for her continuous encouragement and support.

Contents

PREFACE iii

STUDY GUIDE viii

GETTING STARTED WITH WORDPERFECT 6.0 FOR WINDOWS WP1

Starting WordPerfect 6.0 for Windows; What You Will See; Using WordPerfect 6.0 for Windows; Using Menus; Using the Keyboard; Dialog Boxes; Conventions; Storing Your Data; System Requirements; Preferences; Printing Your Documents; Getting Help; WordPerfect for DOS Users; Questions for Review

LESSON 1 Creating Saving and Printing WP13

Insert Current Date; Other Forms of Dates; Save the Document; Print the Document; Using the Power Bar; Close the File; Exit WordPerfect; Exit Windows; Questions for Review; Review Exercise

LESSON 2 Opening, Editing, Undoing, and Undeleting WP23

Opening a Document; Moving through the Document; Editing Text with the Mouse; Using Insert; Editing Text with the Keyboard; Using Typeover; Saving the Document with a Different Name; Zoom; Selecting Text Blocks; Undo; Undelete; Questions for Review; Review Exercises

LESSON 3 Formatting Documents WP39

The Ruler Bar; Displaying the Ruler Bar; Changing the Margins; Setting Tabs; Indenting Text; Page Breaks; Changing Justification; Changing Line Spacing; Questions for Review; Review Exercises

LESSON 4 Reveal Codes, Speller, and Envelope WP55

Reveal Codes; Adjusting the Size of the Reveal Codes Screen; Deleting Codes; Troubleshooting with Reveal Codes; Checking Your Spelling; QuickCorrect; Questions for Review

LESSON 5 **Enhancing Text Appearance** WP67

Fonts; Bold, Italic, and Underline; Making Changes after Keying; Centering; Flush Right; Converting Case (Uppercase/Lowercase); Questions for Review; Review Exercises

LESSON 6 **Editing Features** WP81

Cut, Copy, and Paste; Drag and Drop Text; Find and Replace; Finding a Word, Phrase, or Code; Replacing Text and Codes; Hyphenation; Questions for Review

LESSON 7 **ExpressDocs Templates** WP91

Using Templates; Questions for Review

LESSON 8 **Multi-page Documents and Printing** WP99

Multi-page Documents; Inserting a Document into an Existing Window; Using Page Numbers; Keeping Text Together; Headers and Footers; The Go To Command; Printing; Questions for Review

LESSON 9 **Footnotes, Endnotes, Thesaurus, and Grammatik** WP113

Footnotes and Endnotes; Using the Thesaurus; Using Grammatik; Document Information; Questions for Review; Review Exercise

LESSON 10 **Multiple Windows/Multiple Documents** WP129

Opening More Than One Document; Viewing Multiple Windows; Switching between Documents; Cutting, Copying, and Pasting between Documents; Closing a Document Window; Closing All Documents; Questions for Review

LESSON 11 **Managing Files** WP137

Open File; Viewing a File; Using the File Options; Quickfinder; Quicklist; Questions for Review

LESSON 12 **Tables** WP155

Creating Tables; Editing the Table Structure; Adding Text and Calculating Totals; Deleting a Table; Floating Cells and Spreadsheets; Questions for Review; Review Exercises

LESSON 13 **Columns** WP167
Creating Newspaper Columns; Balanced Newspaper Columns; Creating Parallel Columns; Questions for Review; Review Exercise

LESSON 14 **Merge** WP179
Creating a Data File; Creating a Form File; Printing Letters and Envelopes Using Merge; Performing the Merge Without Envelopes; Performing a Keyboard Merge; Questions for Review; Review Exercises

LESSON 15 **Labels and Sort** WP193
Label Definitions; Creating Labels for Mass Mailings; Sorting; Questions for Review

LESSON 16 **Graphics Borders, Lines, and Boxes** WP201
Graphics Borders; Graphics Lines; Customizing or Editing a Graphics Line; Text Boxes; Questions for Review; Review Exercise

LESSON 17 **TextArt and Graphics Images** WP217
Creating a TextArt Image; Editing TextArt Images; Graphics Images; Editing Graphics Boxes; Editing Graphics Images; Questions for Review

LESSON 18 **Macros** WP231
Creating or Recording a Macro; Playing a Macro; Editing a Macro; Using WordPerfect Macros; Watermark; Questions for Review; Review Exercises

CULMINATING PROJECT WP239
Creating a Flyer

APPENDIX A **Customizing Options** WP241

APPENDIX B **Guide to Troubleshooting with Reveal Codes** WP249

QUICK REFERENCE TO KEYBOARD COMMANDS WP251

INDEX WP253

Study Guide

	Score	Date Completed	Instructor
Lesson 1 Creating, Saving, and Printing			
Lesson 2 Opening, Editing, Undoing, and Undeleting			
Lesson 3 Formatting Documents			
Lesson 4 Reveal Codes, Speller, and Envelope			
Lesson 5 Enhancing Text Appearance			
Lesson 6 Editing Features			
Lesson 7 ExpressDocs Templates			
Lesson 8 Multi-page Documents and Printing			
Lesson 9 Footnotes, Endnotes, Thesaurus, and Grammatik			
Lesson 10 Multiple Windows/Multiple Documents			
Lesson 11 Managing Files			
Lesson 12 Tables			
Lesson 13 Columns			
Lesson 14 Merge			
Lesson 15 Labels and Sort			
Lesson 16 Graphics Borders, Lines, and Boxes			
Lesson 17 TextArt and Graphics Images			
Lesson 18 Macros			
Culminating Project Creating a Flyer			

Getting Started
with WordPerfect 6.0 for Windows

OBJECTIVES

Upon completion of this lesson, you will be able to:

1. Access the WordPerfect 6.0 for Windows software program.
2. Define basic parts of the WordPerfect 6.0 for Windows working screen.
3. Use pull-down menus and dialog boxes.
4. Use the WordPerfect 6.0 for Windows Help features.

STARTING WORDPERFECT FOR WINDOWS

In order to start WordPerfect 6.0 for Windows, your computer must be running the Windows software. If Windows is not running, key win at the DOS prompt (>) and press **Enter**.

After a period of time (this will vary with different systems), you will see a screen titled Program Manager. The WordPerfect program icon (small graphic image) will appear in the Word-Perfect 6.0 program group. (See Figure GS-1.)

Move the mouse pointer (an arrow) onto the WordPerfect 6.0 for Windows icon and double-click (press the left button on the mouse twice in quick succession).

NOTE

See your instructor to learn how to open WordPerfect 6.0 for Windows if you are unable to find the WordPerfect program icon.

Figure GS-1

WHAT YOU WILL SEE

You will see a small hourglass which indicates that WordPerfect 6.0 for Windows is loading. The WordPerfect 6.0 for Windows title screen will appear briefly and will then be replaced by an empty document window.

When you begin, the screen shown in Figure GS-2 will appear. "WordPerfect–[Document1 – unmodified]" will appear in the **Title Bar**. Note the labeled parts:

The **Menu Bar** appears just below the Title Bar. Each item on the Menu Bar is the title of a pull-down menu which will appear when a Menu Bar title is selected.

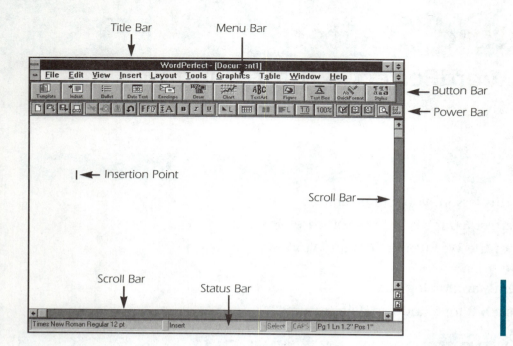

Figure GS-2
WordPerfect 6.0 for Windows opening screen

The **Button Bar** and **Power Bar** that appear just below the Menu Bar provide a series of buttons you can choose from to perform some common actions such as open, save, and print.

The **Insertion Point** is the blinking vertical bar that indicates where text will appear when you key it.

The **Status Bar** at the bottom of the screen indicates where your Insertion Point is located within your document. On the right side of the Status Bar, you can see which page (Pg) you are on, the distance from the top edge of the paper (Ln), and the distance from the left edge of the paper (Pos). Note that these measurements are from the paper's edge—not the margin. The current font is displayed on the left side of the Status Bar. WordPerfect also uses the Status Bar to display information about a feature currently in use.

You can use the **Scroll Bar** at the right side of the screen to scroll (move up and down) to see different parts of your document. You can use the Scroll Bar at the bottom of the screen to scroll right and left.

USING WORDPERFECT 6.0 FOR WINDOWS

There are several methods described below to give commands to WordPerfect 6.0 for Windows. The method you choose is up to you. You may frequently wish to use a combination of methods.

The mouse pointer points to a position on the screen as you move the mouse around on the desktop. The mouse pointer has more than one shape. When the mouse pointer is in the document area, it appears as an **I–beam**. When the mouse pointer is in the area around the document window (such as the Menu Bar), it appears as an **arrow**.

As you work through the lessons in this book, you will be instructed to perform a certain action using your mouse. The following terms are used when you need to perform such actions. They refer to the left mouse button, unless the directions specify the right mouse button.

Click Press and release.

Double–click Click twice in rapid succession.

Drag Press and hold down the mouse button while moving the mouse.

Point Move the mouse until the tip of the mouse pointer rests on the item.

Release Lift your finger from the mouse button.

▶ USING MENUS

WordPerfect 6.0 for Windows provides pull-down menus, as shown in Figure GS-3, that make it easy to find and use various features of the software. Also, you can use the keyboard to access WordPerfect features.

Using the Mouse with Pull-Down Menus

There are two ways to use a mouse for choosing an item from a menu:

Point-and-click method: To select the date using this method, move the mouse pointer to Insert on the Menu Bar and click on the *left* button. (See Figure GS-3 on the next page.) When the menu is displayed, move the mouse pointer to Date and click. When the submenu appears, move the mouse pointer to Date Text and click.

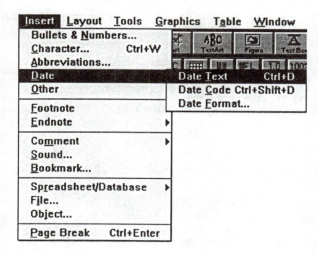

Figure GS-3
Insert pull-down menu

Drag-and-release method: To select the date in this way, move the mouse pointer to Insert on the Menu Bar and hold down the *left* mouse button. Continue holding down the mouse button when the menu is displayed, and then drag the mouse until Date is highlighted and the submenu appears. Drag the mouse to the Date Text option in the submenu and release the mouse button to select the item.

If an option on a menu is *grayed*, it means that it cannot be selected at this time. If you pull down a menu and then decide you do not want it, you can make the menu disappear by pointing the mouse outside the menu and clicking on the left mouse button or by pressing the **Alt** key.

QUICKMENUS

WordPerfect 6.0 for Windows provides a feature known as QuickMenus, which provides QuickMenus related to various locations on the screen by just clicking on the right mouse button. For example, if you are editing text, place the mouse pointer in the text area, click the right mouse button, and a handy QuickMenu appears that includes several basic editing functions.

USING THE KEYBOARD WITH MENUS

You can use the underlined letters as shortcuts to move more quickly through the menus and select an item. For example, to select the date text function, you would begin by pressing **Alt+I** to open the Insert menu, then key D for Date, and then T for Date Text.

There are different ways to use the mouse and the menus. In this exercise, you will use three different methods so that you can become comfortable with some of these different ways. First, practice using the mouse until you know what to do when you read the terms click, double–click, drag, point, and release.

▶ **EXERCISE GS-1**

1. Practice pointing to Insert and clicking on the left mouse button. Move the mouse pointer to Date and click. When the submenu appears, move the mouse pointer to Date Text and click. You should get today's date on the screen. Press **Enter** four times.

2. Move the mouse pointer to Insert on the Menu Bar and hold down the left mouse button. Drag the mouse pointer down until the menu is displayed and until Date is highlighted and the submenu appears. Drag the mouse button to the Date Text option and when it is highlighted, release the mouse button. You should again get today's date on the screen. Press **Enter** four times.

3. Press **Alt+I** to open the insert menu, then key D for Date, and then key T for Date Text. Again, you will get today's date on the screen.

Continue using the mouse and keys until you become comfortable with the several ways you can access the menus. Click on File and look at what is listed on the menu. Then click on Edit and look at what is listed on the menu. Notice that some of the options are grayed. Remember, that means you cannot use those options at this time. Continue clicking on the other options on the Menu Bar and become familiar with their contents. Look at the buttons on the Power Bar and notice that some of those buttons are grayed and cannot be used now.

▶ **EXERCISE GS-2**

▶ USING THE KEYBOARD

Keyboard commands are available for many of the features in WordPerfect 6.0 for Windows. You can find these commands beside the feature on the pull-down menus. They provide a quick method of performing certain steps. For example, the keys **Alt+F4** (where you hold down the Alt key and press the F4 function key) are used to exit.

It is likely that you will want to use a combination of the mouse and keys—whatever is easiest or most comfortable for you.

▶ DIALOG BOXES

A dialog box appears when WordPerfect 6.0 for Windows needs to communicate with the user. It conveys current information about the program, and it may request more information about a particular option. For example, if you ask to open a file, WordPerfect displays the dialog box shown in Figure GS-4 so you can enter the name of the file or choose the file you want from the list of files. The Filenames in your dialog box may differ from those shown here. You will find that dialog boxes have Title Bars that identify the function of the dialog box.

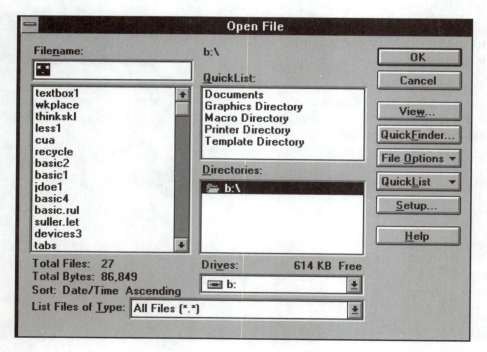

Figure GS-4
Open File dialog box

WP6   GETTING STARTED with WordPerfect for Windows

CONVENTIONS

You will find this book easier to work with if you understand how it is designed to help you learn WordPerfect 6.0 for Windows quickly. First, there are certain conventions (standard procedures) followed throughout the book as to *how* things are laid out for you.

The different typefaces in this manual are used as follows:

Sans Serif type	This typeface is used for the exercises in the lessons. You need to perform actions on the computer only if they are in this typeface.
Monospace type	`This typeface represents text which you are to key.`
Italic	*Italic is used for important information which you should note.*
Bold	**Bold is used for new words, commands, and file names.**

When you see two keys with a plus between them (as in **Alt+F3**) you should hold down the first key and then press the second. When you see two keys with a comma between them (as in **Alt+L, P, S**), you should press the keys one after the other, not simultaneously.

The names of menus and menu options, commands, and dialog boxes are capitalized; for example:

> the File menu
>
> the Print option
>
> the Save As command
>
> the Save As dialog box

The word "key" is used whenever you must type information on the keyboard.

Beginning with Lesson 1, you will be provided with a variety of exercises which you are to perform. Read each exercise carefully for understanding because both the content and practice are important to your learning and understanding of WordPerfect 6.0 for Windows.

This is a self-paced learning book. The speed with which you work through it is up to you. Do not, however, skip any steps because you are likely to need to know them in later lessons. In addition, many lessons build upon one another so that completing one exercise depends on your having successfully completed an earlier one.

▶ STORING YOUR DATA

You must save your work whenever indicated. You will use some of your work in more than one lesson. Your instructor will provide you with instructions as to whether you should store on a hard disk, file server, or your own data disk. If you do use a floppy disk, it should be previously formatted through DOS.

▶ SYSTEM REQUIREMENTS

WordPerfect Corporation recommends the following computer hardware to run WordPerfect 6.0 for Windows efficiently:

IBM or IBM-compatible PC

80486 or higher microprocessor

6–8 megabytes of RAM (temporary memory)

Hard disk with 27M free disk space

Windows 3.1 running in enhanced mode

VGA graphics adapter and monitor

Maintain 4M or more of available disk space for temporary files

Because some WordPerfect features are not accessible from the keyboard, WordPerfect recommends that you use a mouse.

▶ PREFERENCES

WordPerfect allows you to change a number of its default settings using the Preferences command in the File menu. This book assumes that you have *not* changed any settings using the Preferences command.

▶ PRINTING YOUR DOCUMENTS

Your instructor will provide you with information about the printer(s) available to you in your classroom or laboratory and whether you may need to use the Select Printer feature.

▶ GETTING HELP

While in any editing window, pressing **F1** *or* moving the mouse pointer to Help on the Menu Bar and clicking on Help and Contents will cause the Help Contents to appear. (See Figure GS-5.)

This index provides an alphabetical listing of all the topics in the Help files. You can read more about each topic by selecting it from the list. Pressing **F1** while in a dialog box will give general help on that particular topic. This is known as **context-sensitive** help.

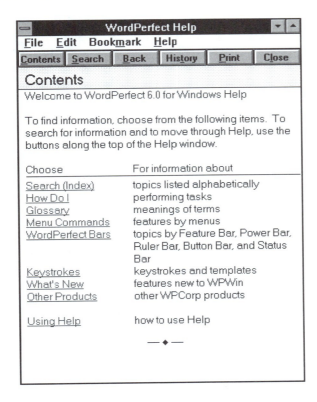

Figure GS-5
Help Contents

COACH

WordPerfect offers a feature called Coach, which will lead you step-by-step through some of WordPerfect's features. To access Coach, just choose Help and then Coach, and the Coach dialog box will appear. The dialog box has a list of the Types of Lessons Available. Using the Coach is a good way to become acquainted with these features. Highlight the type of lesson you want to learn about and a brief description of the feature will appear in the description box. Choose OK and you will be provided with more information. Then you can click on either Continue, if you want more information, or Skip this Coach to quit using Coach.

HELP PROMPTS

WordPerfect offers brief Help prompts or descriptions when you place the mouse pointer on any of the icons on the Button Bar or Power Bar. For example, place the mouse pointer on the button which says Indent. In the Title Bar, the description "Indent—Indent the current paragraph one tab stop–F7" will appear. Place the mouse pointer on the Power Bar button which has a B on it, and in the Title Bar, the description "Bold Font–Turn on Bold Font–Ctrl+B" will appear. In these examples, **F7** and **Ctrl+B** are the CUA keystrokes to use these features.

Practice using some of the Help features provided by WordPerfect 6.0 for Windows:

▶ **EXERCISE GS-3**

1. Press **F1** OR move the mouse pointer to Help on the Menu Bar and click. Then click on Contents and the Help Contents will appear.

2. Click on Using Help and read how to use Help. Then click on the Close button.

3. Click again on Help and Contents, then on Keystrokes, and notice the list of CUA and DOS keystrokes for moving around in WordPerfect 6.0 for Windows. Click on the Close button. Look at any other parts of the contents you wish.

4. Click on Help and then on Coach to look at the Coach dialog box. Notice the contents and double-click on any you want to read now. Then click on Quit when you are through.

5. Move the mouse pointer up to the Power Bar onto the button with the letter B. Notice that a Help prompt about Bold will appear at the top of the screen when you first place the mouse pointer on the button. Now move the mouse pointer to U and you will see a Help prompt about Underline. Move your mouse pointer to more of the buttons on both the Power Bar and Button Bar to see more Help prompts.

▶ WORDPERFECT FOR DOS USERS

If you use WordPerfect 6.0 for DOS, you will find that WordPerfect 6.0 for Windows is similar. What you do in WordPerfect 6.0 for DOS, you can probably do in WordPerfect 6.0 for Windows. Documents created with either program can be used interchangeably, with no conversion required.

If you are used to WordPerfect 6.0 for DOS, you may find yourself wanting to press Enter after you key text in a dialog box. In WordPerfect 6.0 for Windows, pressing Enter in a dialog box usually accepts all the default selections or changes you have made and closes the box. If there are items you need to check in that box, make sure that you don't press Enter until after you have filled out the *whole* box.

REVIEW

TRUE/FALSE

Circle the correct answer.

1. T F   A small hourglass appears on the screen when WordPerfect 6.0 for Windows is loading.

2. T F   Both the Button Bar and Power Bar provide a series of buttons you can choose from to perform some common WordPerfect actions.

3. T F   The mouse pointer has more than one shape.

4. T F   To obtain context–sensitive help, you must press F1 while in a dialog box.

5. T F   Documents created with either WordPerfect 6.0 for DOS or WordPerfect 6.0 for Windows are interchangeable.

6. T F   WordPerfect provides a feature called Coach, which offers brief prompts or descriptions when you place the mouse pointer on any of the buttons on the Power Bar or Button Bar.

COMPLETION

Fill in the blank.

1. If Windows is not running, key _____ at the DOS prompt and press Enter.

2. When you begin, "WordPerfect-[Document1-unmodified]" will appear in the _____ _____ .

3. The _____ _____ at the right side of the screen is used to move up and down through your document.

4. A _____ _____ conveys current information about the program, and it may request information about a particular option.

5. To get help, press _____ or move the mouse pointer to Help on the Menu Bar.

6. The _____ _____ is the blinking vertical bar in the active document window which indicates where text will appear when you key it.

REFERENCE QUESTION:

Look at the WordPerfect 6.0 for Windows Reference Manual or User's Guide documentation, if available. The table of contents is made up of five major parts. List the parts and briefly describe the contents of each.

LESSON 1

Creating, Saving, and Printing

OBJECTIVES

Upon completion of this lesson, you will be able to:

1. Insert a date into a document.
2. Create a basic document using WordPerfect 6.0 for Windows.
3. Save and print documents using WordPerfect 6.0 for Windows.
4. Close a file.
5. Use the Power Bar.
6. Exit both WordPerfect 6.0 for Windows and Windows.

Because a document window is opened automatically when you start WordPerfect, you can begin to key your document immediately. If you accidentally key an error, you can backspace to correct it. Backspace erases text to the left of the Insertion Point one character or space at a time.

INSERT CURRENT DATE

The current date can be inserted most quickly by clicking the mouse pointer on the Date Text button on the Button Bar (the group of icon buttons immediately below the Menu Bar). This date will not change unless you edit it.

OTHER FORMS OF DATES

You can also place the current date in your document if you:

- Choose Insert and Date.

The Insert/Date menu is shown in Figure 1-1. The Date Text option places the current date in your document at the Insertion Point, just as if you had keyed it. The date you inserted does not change unless you edit it.

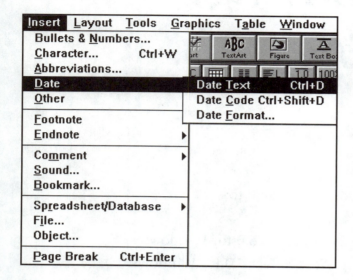

Figure 1-1
Insert/Date menu

The Date Code option places the current date in your document, but every time you open or print the document, the date is changed to reflect the current date.

The Date Format can be used to change the way the date appears. When you choose Date Format, a dialog box appears which offers you a variety of date formats from which to choose; or you can click on Custom and customize the date format.

Insert the current date by clicking on the Date Text icon on the Button Bar. Key the paragraphs shown in Figure 1-2. Use the **Backspace** *key to correct any errors as you key. You should not press the* **Enter** *key at the end of each line because of the* **auto wordwrap** *feature which wraps the text to the next line automatically. Press* **Enter** *only at the ends of paragraphs and to leave blank lines. Key your own name where "Your Name" is indicated. Your line endings may be slightly different because of the way Word-Perfect 6.0 for Windows works with your printer.*

▶ **EXERCISE 1-1**

```
Current Date

Welcome to WordPerfect for Windows. With this program
you get all the power and versatility of the
WordPerfect program with the attractive and user-
friendly Windows graphical environment.

When WordPerfect first comes on, the screen is blank,
similar to a blank piece of paper in a typewriter. If
you want to insert the current date, you can do so
quickly by clicking on the Date Text icon on the Button
Bar. To prepare the remainder of your document, you
simply begin typing.

If you make any mistakes as you type, you can erase
them by simply backspacing over them and then
continuing as if the mistakes had never been made.

Saving a document is as easy as choosing Save from the
File menu and naming the file. (Starting printing works
the same way by your choosing Print from the File
menu).

You also have the option of using a Power Bar when you
use WordPerfect. Several of the more commonly used menu
items such as Open, Save, and Print (which you will
learn about in this lesson) are listed on the default
Power Bar so you don't have to pick them from a menu,
but can instead click on the button with the mouse to
execute a command more quickly.

Your Name
```

Figure 1-2

WordPerfect is designed to help you create documents easily. The creators of the software built some predetermined settings, called **defaults**, into the software so that you can set up many documents very quickly. Some of the defaults are:

Margins are set at one inch all around your document (top, bottom, right, and left). Margins are measured from the edges of a page.

Tabs are set at every one-half inch.

Line spacing is set for single.

SAVE THE DOCUMENT

When you create documents on your computer, all your work is stored temporarily in the computer's memory. If you turn off your computer, all your work will be lost. For this reason, you need to save your work to a disk so that you can retrieve and reuse it at a later date. To do this, you will need to use WordPerfect's Save feature.

In order to save a file, you must give it a name. File names may consist of two parts separated by a period. The first part, called the file name, consists of one to eight letters or digits; the second part, which is optional, is called the extension and can have up to three letters or digits. WordPerfect 6.0 for Windows will add the extension **.wpd** if you do not specify an extension. (See Figure 1-3.)

If you are learning in a classroom or laboratory, your instructor will tell you where and how you should save your documents. Students usually save on their own disks, in Drive A or Drive B, so that they don't save their documents on the hard disk (Drive C).

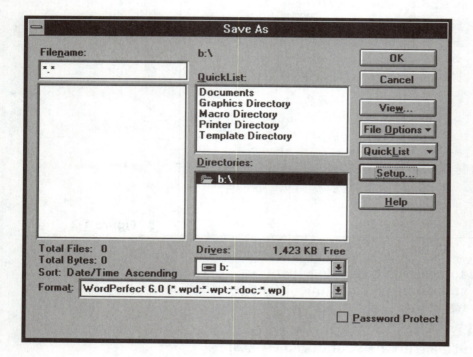

Figure 1-3
Save As dialog box

To save a file:

- Choose File and then Save.
- Key the name of your file in the Filename text box.
- Click on OK to save the file.

The Save As dialog box will appear the first time you save the file. However, if you select the Save command after a file has been named, you will not be given the Save As dialog box. WordPerfect will save over (replace) the previous file and you will lose the first file. You *must* use Save As in order to have two separate files.

Save the document you created in Exercise 1. Key the name **less1**. Your instructor will tell you where to save this lesson. Do not Close the file yet.

▶ **EXERCISE 1-2**

PRINT THE DOCUMENT

You can use WordPerfect's Print command to print a copy of your on–screen document. The quality of your output will vary, depending on the type of printer you have attached to your computer.

To begin the printing process:

- Choose File and then Print *or* press **F5**.

You may have more than one printer to select from. The current printer will be displayed near the top of the Print dialog box shown in Figure 1-4. If you want to use a different printer, click on Select. The Select Printer dialog box will appear. Highlight the printer you want and click on Select. This printer should then be displayed on the Print dialog box.

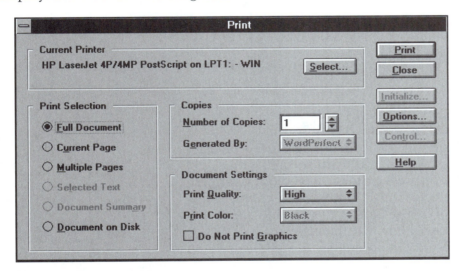

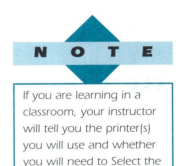

N O T E

If you are learning in a classroom, your instructor will tell you the printer(s) you will use and whether you will need to Select the printer.

Figure 1-4
Print dialog box

Finally, click on Print (in the upper right corner of the dialog box) or press **Enter** to print the file.

 Print the document **less1**.

▶ **EXERCISE 1-3**

USE THE POWER BAR

The WordPerfect Power Bar™ is a bar of icon buttons which is located immediately above the WordPerfect editing screen. The Power Bar lets you quickly access frequently used menu commands with your mouse.

The default Power Bar (See Figure 1-5 on the next page.) will appear automatically when you access WordPerfect. Some commands are grayed because they cannot be used until some other action has taken place.

Figure 1-5
Default Power Bar

Here's how you might use the Power Bar to perform a few basic tasks more quickly.

To save the file, move the mouse pointer to the Save button and click. Clicking the Save button on the Power Bar will save the document (if it has been saved before) without prompting you to confirm that you want to save it under the same name. An hourglass will appear on the screen while the document is being saved. If the file hasn't been saved before, the Save As dialog box will be displayed automatically.

To print the file, move the mouse pointer to the Print button and click. The Print dialog box will appear quickly. Move the mouse pointer to the Print command in the upper right corner of the box and click.

See Appendix A for how you can customize the Power Bar to contain those functions which you perform most frequently.

CLOSE THE FILE

To close a file:

- Choose File and then Close, *or* press **Ctrl+F4**.

If you have made any changes to your document since the last time you saved, you will be asked if you want to save your changes. You can select Yes or press **Enter** to save your changes and close the document, select No to not save your changes and still close your document, or select Cancel to not save your changes and return to the document without closing.

Practice using the Power Bar to Save and Print the exercise you named **less1** in Exercise 1-2. Finally, Close the document.

▶ **EXERCISE 1-4**

EXIT WORDPERFECT

To exit WordPerfect:

- Choose File and then Exit.

Choosing Exit from the File menu exits you from WordPerfect and returns you to the Windows Program Manager. You are given a chance to save any documents you haven't saved yet.

Now that you have learned how to use the mouse and menus, the keyboard, the Button Bar, and the Power Bar, you can select the method you prefer to perform various functions.

EXIT WINDOWS

You should always exit Windows before turning off the system.

To exit Windows:

- Choose File on the Program Manager menu, and then choose Exit Windows.

The Exit Windows dialog box will appear. Choose OK.

Exit WordPerfect and Exit Windows by following the steps given in the previous section, unless you are going on to the next lesson.

EXERCISE 1-5

Congratulations! You have now learned how to create, save, and print a simple document—as well as how to load and exit WordPerfect and Windows.

REVIEW

TRUE/FALSE

Circle the correct answer.

1. T F Because a document window is opened automatically when you start WordPerfect, you can begin to key your document immediately.

2. T F If you select the Save command after a file has been named, the file will be saved immediately with the original file name.

3. T F If you wish to save a document with a new name, you should use the Save feature.

4. T F The quality of your printing output will vary, depending on the type of printer you have attached to your computer.

5. T F When you Exit WordPerfect, you are given a chance to save any documents you haven't saved yet.

6. T F The default margins are one inch from the top, bottom, left, and right edges of the paper.

COMPLETION

Fill in the blank.

1. To change the way a date appears, choose Insert, Date, and _____ _____.

2. With the _____ _____ option, the date is changed to reflect the current date every time you open or print the document.

3. File names consist of two parts separated by a period. The first part, called the file name, consists of one to eight letters or digits; the second part is called the extension and can have up to _____ letters or digits.

4. When you Save a file that has never been saved before, the _____ _____ dialog box will appear.

5. If you have more than one printer to print from, you must _____ the correct printer.

6. When commands are _____, they cannot be used until some other action has taken place.

Reference Question: Look at the WordPerfect 6.0 for Windows Troubleshooting section in the Appendix of the Reference Manual or User's Guide. Look at the contents of this section and find the Cause and Solution to the following Problem and write them in the space below.

When I choose Save from the File menu, I am not asked whether I want to save with a different name.

REVIEW EXERCISE

Periodically throughout this book, you will find some review exercises which are designed to reinforce the skills you have learned in previous lessons. Instructions are given for each exercise. See if you can complete the exercises without having to refer to the lessons.

Key the text in Figure 1-6. Leave a blank line between paragraphs by pressing **Enter** twice. Use **Tab** to indent the first line of each paragraph. Insert the date as a code at the end of the document using the format shown. Save this document with the name **keyboard**. Print one copy. Close the file.

▶ **REVIEW EXERCISE 1-1**

```
     WordPerfect for Windows takes advantage of the
graphical nature of the Windows interface. You will see
how your document looks and, as you edit it, most
changes you make will be instantly visible. With the
Button Bar and Power Bar displayed on screen, WordPerfect
offers a range of powerful editing and text manipulation
features that help to simplify and speed up document
preparation.

     CUA stands for Common User Access and is the name of
the design standard used to give various Windows
software programs a similar look and feel. The CUA
standard governs the design of pull-down menus, dialog
boxes, windows, and keyboard layouts.

     WordPerfect for Windows incorporates these standards
in its overall design and includes a default keyboard
that corresponds to the CUA guidelines.

     Why learn CUA keystrokes?  The most important reason
for learning the Common User Access keyboard is
compatibility with other Windows-based programs. As you
purchase more and more software, you will find that most
Windows applications use the CUA standard. If you know a
fair number of the CUA keystrokes, your transition from
one Windows application to another will be much easier.

     WordPerfect for Windows also supports a DOS keyboard
which helps people make the transition from an older
version of WordPerfect and become more productive more
quickly.

4/15/95
```

Figure 1-6

LESSON 2

Opening, Editing, Undo, and Undelete

OBJECTIVES

Upon completion of this lesson, you will be able to:

1. Open a document.
2. Move through the document using the mouse and keystrokes.
3. Edit previously keyed contents—Delete and Insert or use Typeover to make changes and corrections.
4. Save a document with a different name.
5. Use Zoom.
6. Select text blocks.
7. Undo and Undelete deletions previously made.

OPENING A DOCUMENT

When you are ready to work with a document that you have saved previously with WordPerfect, you must first "open" it. If the current document window is empty (as is the case when you first start WordPerfect), the document will be opened there. If the current window already contains a document, a new window will be opened. You will learn how to work with multiple document windows in Lesson 10.

- Click on the Open icon on the Power Bar, *or*
- Choose File and then Open from the menu.

The Open File dialog box will appear. (See Figure 2-1 on the next page.) Double-click on the name of your file or highlight the file you want to open, and press **Enter** or click on OK to open the file.

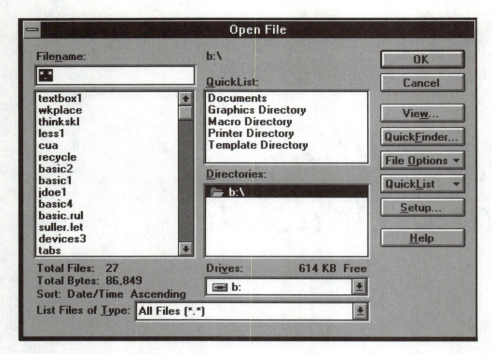

Figure 2-1
Open File dialog box

You can also key the name of the document file you want to open in the Filename text box.

MOVING THROUGH THE DOCUMENT

You can use either the mouse or the keyboard to move through the document. The mouse uses the Scroll Bar to move the screen, while the keystrokes move the Insertion Point. If you wish to edit text after moving the screen with the mouse, you must move back onto the editing screen and click with the mouse where you wish the Insertion Point to appear.

USING THE SCROLL BAR

WordPerfect has horizontal and vertical Scroll Bars that let you use the mouse to move through the document. (See Figure 2-2 on the next page.) When you move using the Scroll Bars, the text scrolls but the Insertion Point does not move.

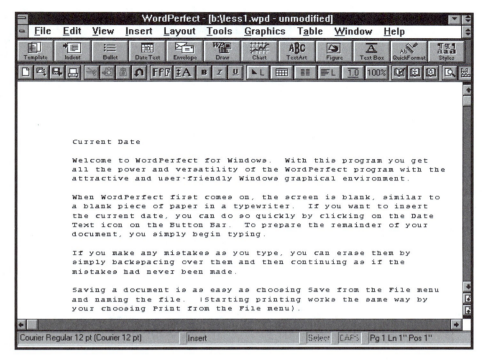

Figure 2-2
Use the Scroll Bars to move text.

You can use the Scroll Bar at the right side of the screen to scroll through your document. If you click on the Scroll Bar several times, the text scrolls down one screen each time you click the Scroll Bar.

You can also place the mouse pointer over the scroll box and drag it down by holding down the left mouse button. If you move the scroll box to the top, the screen will scroll to the top of the document. If you move the scroll box about halfway, the screen will scroll about halfway through the document.

At the very bottom of the vertical bar, you will see up and down arrows on small pages. If you click on the up arrow page, the screen will roll up a page; if you click on the down arrow page, the screen will roll down a page.

USING KEYSTROKES

You can also move through the document quickly with a variety of keystrokes for moving the Insertion Point through the document. (See Table 2-1 on the next page.)

Keystrokes	Result
↑ ↓	Move up or down one line.
→ ←	Move right or left one character.
Home	Move to the beginning of the line.
End	Move to the end of the line.
Ctrl+Home	Go to the top of the document.
Ctrl+End	Go to the bottom of the document.
Page Up	Move up one screen.
Page Down	Move down one screen.

Table 2-1
Keystrokes for Moving through the Document

Now that you are familiar with using both the Scroll Bar and keystrokes, you can choose whichever method seems better to you for a particular situation.

▶ **EXERCISE 2-1**

Open the file called **less1.wpd**. Note that because you did not specify an extension when you saved it, WordPerfect 6.0 for Windows has added the .wpd extension. Practice moving through the document with both the Scroll Bar and the keystrokes given in the table.

EDITING TEXT WITH THE MOUSE

In order to edit text with the mouse, all you need to do is move the I–beam to the location that you want to edit and click. The Insertion Point will appear and you can make corrections by pressing the **Backspace** key to erase characters to the *left* of the Insertion Point or the **Delete** key to erase characters to the *right* of the Insertion Point.

USING INSERT

When you key text in WordPerfect, the text appears at the Insertion Point and existing text is pushed forward. To insert additional text, simply key the new characters and they will appear at the Insertion Point.

> **EXERCISE 2-2**

Continuing with **less1.wpd**, practice the steps given below to learn how to use the mouse to delete previously keyed contents, and to insert letters, spaces, and words into already keyed text.

1. Using the mouse, move the Insertion Point to just before the word `graphical` at the end of the first paragraph and click.
2. Press **Delete** <u>TEN</u> times in order to erase the word `graphical` and the space.
3. Press **Backspace** <u>EIGHT</u> times in order to erase the word `Windows`.
4. Key the letters `GUI` at the Insertion Point. (Add a space, if necessary.)

EDITING TEXT WITH THE KEYBOARD

Editing text with the keyboard is as simple as using the keystrokes shown in Table 2-1 to move the Insertion Point to the text you want to edit. You can then press **Backspace** or **Delete** to erase characters or add letters by simply keying at the Insertion Point.

> **EXERCISE 2-3**

Practice the steps given below to use the keyboard to delete previously keyed contents, and to insert letters, spaces, and words into already keyed text.

1. Use the arrow keys to move the Insertion Point just before the word `screen` in the second paragraph. Press the **Backspace** key until you erase the word `the`.
2. With your Insertion Point in the same location, key the word `your`. (Add a space, if necessary.)

USING TYPEOVER

You can choose to key over existing text. Double-click on the word "Insert" on the Status Bar at the bottom of the screen or press the **Insert (Ins)** key to change from Insert to Typeover.

> **EXERCISE 2-4**

Practice the steps given below to use the keyboard to delete previously keyed contents, and to use the Typeover mode to edit your document. Use the mouse or keystrokes to move the Insertion Point to the text you want to edit.

1. Place the Insertion Point just before the letter `o` in `option` in the first line of the last paragraph.
2. Press the **Insert (Ins)** key to begin Typeover. Note the word "Typeover" in the center of the Status Bar at the bottom of the screen.
3. Key `choice` over `option`.
4. Press **Insert (Ins)** again to turn off Typeover.

SAVING THE DOCUMENT WITH A DIFFERENT NAME

After you've edited a file, you will want to save the new version. If you want to keep the original version intact on disk you *must* save the new one with a different name. (See Figure 2-3.)

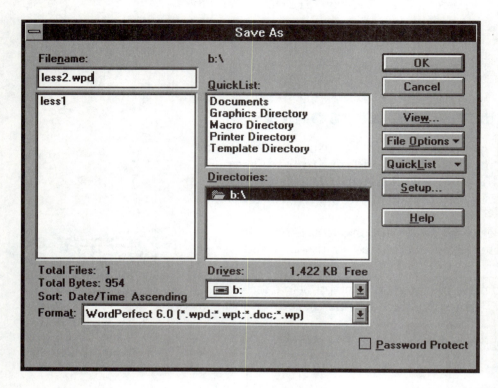

Figure 2-3
Save As dialog box

- Select Save As from the File menu. Key the name of your new file at the blinking Insertion Point. Click on OK to save the file or press **Enter**.

Use the Save As command to save this document as **less2.wpd**. Then Close the document.

▶ **EXERCISE 2-5**

ZOOM

By seeing how your document will be printed before it's actually printed, you can save paper and correct layout problems. You can click on the Page Zoom Full button on the Power Bar to see a miniature of the full page. You can return to your regular screen merely by clicking on this button again.

WP28   **LESSON 2**   OPENING, EDITING, UNDO, AND UNDELETE

The Zoom button on the Power Bar will change the size of the view. Click on the Zoom icon with the left mouse button and hold it down; a drop-down menu will appear. You will be offered a choice of percentages; *or* if you select Other, you can specify a zoom percentage.

▶ **EXERCISE 2-6**

To experiment with Zoom, you should open **less2.wpd**.

1. Click on the Page Zoom icon to see how the page looks.
2. Click on the Zoom icon to increase the size to 150%; then reduce the size to 50% to see more of the page and detail. Return the page to 100%.
3. Close the document without resaving it.

SELECTING TEXT BLOCKS

WordPerfect allows you to Select (highlight) a block of text so that you can perform various functions on it. This process can speed the editing process considerably. Figure 2-4 shows how Selected text is highlighted.

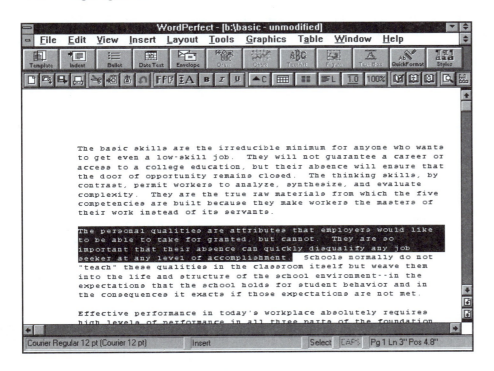

Figure 2-4
Selected text is highlighted.

Note the differences in the following methods:

The quickest and easiest way is to move the Insertion Point to where you want to begin the Selected block, press and hold the left mouse button, and then drag the mouse to where you want to end the block. Sometimes it is hard to be precise with this method.

You can be more precise when you place the Insertion Point anywhere in the text you want to select and choose Se lect from the Edit menu, and then choose Sentence, Paragraph, Page, or All. You can also click the right mouse button anywhere in the left margin to obtain a QuickMenu, and then choose Select Sentence, Select Paragraph, Select Page, or Select All.

To cancel a highlighted selection, click the mouse anywhere outside the selected material.

► **EXERCISE 2-7**

1. Key the document shown in Figure 2-5. Save it with the name **basic**. Do NOT Close this document.

```
The basic skills are the irreducible minimum for
anyone who wants to get even a low-skill job.  They
will not guarantee a career or access to a college
education, but their absence will ensure that the door
of opportunity remains closed.  The thinking skills,
by contrast, permit workers to analyze, synthesize,
and evaluate complexity.  They are the true raw
materials from which the five competencies are built
because they make workers the masters of their work
instead of its servants.

The personal qualities are attributes that employers
would like to be able to take for granted, but cannot.
They are so important that their absence can quickly
disqualify any job seeker at any level of
accomplishment.  Schools normally do not "teach" these
qualities in the classroom itself but weave them into
the life and structure of the school environment--in
the expectations that the school holds for student
behavior and in the consequences it exacts if those
expectations are not met.

Effective performance in today's workplace absolutely
requires high levels of performance in all three parts
of the foundation.  There is no point in belaboring
the obvious.  People who cannot read, write, and
communicate cannot be trusted in a transcription
service.

The rude salesman who alienates customers will not
make sales.  The cashier with a hand in the till
cheats the business and ultimately the customers.
The electrician who cannot solve technical problems
threatens the production line.  Restaurant owners who
cannot creatively approach problems will probably not
be in business for long.

(The preceding material is an excerpt from A SCANS
Report for America 2000 published by the Secretary's
Commission on Achieving Necessary Skills, U.S.
Department of Labor.)
```

▍ Figure 2-5

2. Using the mouse with the drag method, Select the first sentence of the fourth paragraph, beginning with `The rude salesman`, and press **Delete**. Save the document as **basic1**. Remember, you must use Save <u>A</u>s so that WordPerfect does not save this file over **basic**. Do <u>NOT</u> Close this document.

3. Move the Insertion Point to `The personal qualities` at the beginning of the second paragraph. Choose <u>E</u>dit, <u>S</u>elect, and <u>S</u>entence to Select the sentence, and then press **Delete**. Save the document as **basic2**. Remember, you must use Save <u>A</u>s so that WordPerfect does not save over the document named **basic1**. Do <u>NOT</u> Close this document.

With the WordPerfect 6.0a for Windows revision, **QuickSelect** has been added to give you even more *precise* control in Selecting the text you need. Click twice on a word, holding the mouse button down on the last click, and then drag to Select word by word. Click three times, holding the mouse button down on the last click, and then drag to Select sentence by sentence; and click four times and drag to Select paragraph by paragraph.

Once material is Selected or highlighted, you can delete it by merely pressing the **Delete** key. You can also delete quickly by positioning the Insertion Point and using the following keystrokes:

Ctrl+Delete   Delete to the end of the line.

Ctrl+Backspace   Delete word.

Shift+Ctrl+Delete Delete to end of current page.

▶ **EXERCISE 2-8**

1. Move the Insertion Point to the word `The` before the word `cashier` in the first sentence of the fourth paragraph, click twice, and drag to Select the rest of the words in that sentence. Press **Delete**. Move the Insertion Point to `The electrician` at the beginning of the paragraph, click three times, and drag to Select that sentence and the next sentence. Press **Delete**. Move the Insertion Point to the beginning of the third paragraph, beginning with `Effective`. Click four times to Select the paragraph. Press **Delete**. Save the document as **basic3**. Do <u>NOT</u> Close this document.

2. Using the arrow keys, move the Insertion Point to `They` at the beginning of the second paragraph. Press **Ctrl+Backspace** to delete the word. Then move the Insertion Point immediately before the words `job seeker`. Press **Ctrl+Delete** to delete to the end of the line. Move the Insertion Point before the beginning parenthesis at the bottom of the page, and press **Shift+Ctrl+Delete** to delete the remainder of the page. Save the document as **basic4**. Do <u>NOT</u> Close this document.

As you have learned, there is quite a difference in these various methods of Selecting and Deleting. You must choose what you can do most quickly and easily!

UNDO

If you are editing a document and discover that you just made a mistake such as pressing the wrong key, you can undo your error quickly and easily by using WordPerfect's Undo command, Edit, Undo. The Undo command reverses the *last* editing change you made to your document.

You can use Undo or Undelete to restore text that you just accidentally deleted. Undo will restore the text in its *original location*.

It is important that you choose Undo *immediately* if you want to Undo a command. For example, if you delete some text, add some new text, and then choose Undo, the original text will not be restored, but the new text will be removed because inserting the new text was the last editing change made to the document. You can, however, still restore the original text by using the Undelete command.

To use the Undo command, click on the Undo button on the Power Bar *or* click on the Edit menu and then on Undo. You can also key **Ctrl+Z** to Undo.

The last editing change you made was the deletion of the material in parentheses. Undo this change now. Save this document as **basic5**. Close the document.

▶ **EXERCISE 2-9**

UNDELETE

If you mistakenly delete text or codes in WordPerfect, you may be able to restore your material. WordPerfect stores your last three deletions in memory. You can use the Undelete command to restore any of these last three deletions. Undelete can restore text, codes, or a combination of the two.

Limitation: Undelete will not undelete content which you merely forgot to save or that is lost when the computer is turned off or loses power.

When you use Undelete, the text will appear *where your Insertion Point is currently located*. If you want to restore the text to the same place that you deleted it from, you must position your Insertion Point where you want the text restored.

- Choose Edit and Undelete to display the Undelete dialog box. (see Figure 2-6.)

Figure 2-6
Undelete dialog box

You may need to move the Undelete dialog box if it is covering the information you want to restore. You can do this by dragging the Title Bar on the dialog box to a new position.

- Choose Edit, Undelete, and Restore to restore the last deleted text at the Insertion Point *or* move the Insertion Point to the proper place and choose Edit, Undelete, Previous, or Next to cycle through your last three deletions. Then choose Restore when you see the one you want to Undelete.

In this exercise, you will practice using various methods of Delete and Undelete.

1. Open the file named **basic**.
2. Position the Insertion Point at the beginning of the first sentence in the second paragraph, beginning with `The personal`. Click the right mouse button anywhere in the left margin to obtain the QuickMenu and choose Select Sentence. Press **Delete**.
3. Position the Insertion Point at the beginning of the third paragraph, starting with `Effective,` and press **Ctrl+Delete** to delete the first line of the paragraph.
4. Position the Insertion Point on the word `rude` in the first sentence of the fourth paragraph. Press **Ctrl+Backspace** to delete the word. Save this file as **basic6**. Do not Close the document. Remember, with Undelete, you must position the Insertion Point where you want the text restored.
5. Because you just deleted `rude`, the Insertion Point should be in the right place, so now you can use Edit, Undelete, and Restore to place the last deleted text at the Insertion Point.
6. Move the Insertion Point to the proper place at the beginning of the third paragraph and use Edit, Undelete, Previous, and then Restore.
7. Move the Insertion Point to the proper place at the beginning of the second paragraph to Undelete what was the first sentence. Choose Edit, Undelete, and Previous or Next until you see the line beginning with `The Personal`, and then choose Restore.
8. You do not need to Save this file. Close the document.

Key the paragraph in Figure 2-7 exactly as it appears. Do NOT bold the words shown in bold, but key the errors in the words exactly as they are shown. Press **Tab** to indent the first line of each paragraph. Do not press **Enter** at the ends of the lines, but do press **Enter** twice at the end of each paragraph. Save this document and name it **devices1**.

When you have completed keying and saving the paragraph, correct the misspelled words shown in bold using the **Delete** and **Backspace** keys, whichever is most appropriate for the situation. Save the corrected document as **devices2**. Close the document.

> They **well** put Dick Tracy's two-way wrist radio **two** shame. **Evene** Captain Kirk would be **impresed**.
>
> Due **our** next year, these **pocket-sised** devices are a **cros** between a **cellar** phone, fax **machinne**, Rolodex, and **computre**. About the size of a **vidotape**, they have been called **personel** communicators, personal **degitle** assistants or-- perhaps most cleverly--information **applances**.

▌ Figure 2-7

▶ **EXERCISE 2-11**

REVIEW

TRUE/FALSE

Circle the correct answer.

1. T F The mouse uses the Scroll Bar to move the screen, while keystrokes move the Insertion Point.

2. T F WordPerfect defaults to Typeover mode.

3. T F If you want to keep the original version of a document intact after revising it, you must save the new version with a different name.

4. T F To perform various functions on a block of text, you must Select the block of text.

5. T F To see a full page of how your document will be printed, click on the Zoom icon and 200%.

6. T F You can use the Undelete command to restore your last three deletions.

COMPLETION

Fill in the blank.

1. When you are ready to work with a document that you have saved previously with WordPerfect, you must _____ it.

2. Keystrokes actually move the _____ _____.

3. Press the _____ key to erase characters to the left of the Insertion Point or press the _____ key to erase characters to the right of the Insertion Point.

4. Press the _____ key to begin Typeover mode.

5. To save a document with a different name, you must use the _____ _____ command.

6. The _____ command reverses the last editing change you made to your document.

Reference Question: Look in the Appendix of the Reference Manual or User's Guide to find the section on Troubleshooting. Notice the contents of this section and find the Cause and Solution for the following Problem and write them below.

When I use the Scroll Bars to scroll, the Insertion Point disappears.

REVIEW EXERCISES

Key the letter in Figure 2-8 according to the following instructions.

Insert the date, and then press **Enter** four times. Key the inside address and salutation, press **Enter** once after each line, and press **Enter** twice before and after the salutation. Press **Enter** four times before `Credit Manager` in the signature. Put your own reference initials in place of `yrs`. Proofread your document and correct any errors you find. Save this letter as **jwill1** and Print a copy. Close the file.

▶ **REVIEW EXERCISE 2-1**

```
Current Date
(Insert 3 blank lines)
Mr. John Williams
123 West High Street
Freedom, IN 47431

Dear Mr. Williams:

What do you think we should do?

We have a small account that remains unpaid.  We want
to keep the good will of all our customers; yet we
cannot continue to build up large collection expenses.
What do you suggest we do?

This small account, which is yours, is six weeks
overdue.  You know the value of our credit privilege.
Our summer sales will soon place a wide selection of
fine bargains on our shelves, and you will find your
credit with us a valuable convenience.

Our extension of time on your account has already
been most liberal.  Why not settle this account at
once and retain your good credit standing?

I am enclosing an addressed, postage-free envelope for
your convenience.  Please make use of it now to send
us your check.  It will be appreciated.

Sincerely yours,

(Insert 3 blank lines)

Credit Manager

yrs

Enclosure
```

▌ Figure 2-8

REVIEW EXERCISE 2-2

In this exercise, you will revise the body of the letter you saved in Review Exercise 2-1. Open the file named **jwill1** and make the changes shown in Figure 2-9. Save this revision as **jwill2**. Close the file.

```
What do you think we should do?

We have a small account that remains unpaid.  We want
to keep the good will of all our customers; yet we
cannot continue to build up a large collection expense.
What do you suggest we do?

This small account, which is yours, is six weeks
overdue.  You know the value of our credit privilege.
Our summer sales will soon place a wide selection of
fine bargains on our shelves, and you will find your
credit with us a valuable convenience.

Our extension of time on your account has already been
most liberal.  Why not settle this account at once and
retain your good credit standing?

I am enclosing an addressed, postage-free envelope for
your convenience.  Please make use of it now to send
us your check.  It will be appreciated. If we don't
receive payment or hear from you within one
week, we will be forced to turn this matter
over to a collection agency.
```

Figure 2-9

REVIEW EXERCISE 2-3

In this letter, revise the body of the letter you saved in Review Exercise 2-1. Open the file named **jwill1** and make the changes shown in Figure 2-10. Save this revision as **jwill3**. Close the file.

```
What do you think we should do?

We have a small account that remains unpaid.  We want
to keep the good will of all our customers; yet we
cannot continue to build up a large collection expense.
What do you suggest we do?

This small account, which is yours, is ten six weeks
overdue.  You know the value of our credit privilege.
Our summer sales will soon place a wide selection of
fine bargains on our shelves, and you will find your
credit with us a valuable convenience.

Our extension of time on your account has already
been most liberal.  Why not settle this account at once
and retain your good credit standing. Payment must be made
within 30 days to retain a good credit standing with our Credit Department.
I am enclosing an addressed, postage-free envelope for
your convenience.  Please make use of it now to send us
your check.  It will be appreciated.
```

Figure 2-10

WP38 LESSON 2 OPENING, EDITING, UNDO, AND UNDELETE

LESSON 3

Formatting Documents

OBJECTIVES

Upon completion of this lesson, you will be able to:

1. Display the Ruler Bar.
2. Change margins using the Ruler Bar or menus.
3. Change tab settings using the Ruler Bar or menus.
4. Use Indent.
5. Understand the View settings.
6. Create a hard page break.
7. Change justification and line spacing using the Power Bar or menus.

THE RULER BAR

WordPerfect 6.0 for Windows provides a feature known as the Ruler Bar, which allows the user to have easy access to WordPerfect's margins and tabs. You will find the Ruler Bar to be a quick and easy alternative to choosing (with the mouse) certain commands found on the Layout menu.

Any changes that you make take place at the beginning of the paragraph in which the Insertion Point is located. The Ruler Bar displays a graphic representation of the document margins and tab settings. It allows you to click and drag the margin and tab markers in order to change the settings.

DISPLAYING THE RULER BAR

To display the Ruler Bar:

- Choose View and then Ruler Bar.

To remove the Ruler Bar from the document window, repeat this step.

A check mark on the View menu beside the Ruler Bar indicates that the Ruler Bar is on. The WordPerfect Ruler Bar is similar to a ruler that you would use at your desk and is marked in inches.

You can use the Ruler Bar, shown in Figure 3-1, to change margins and tab positions.

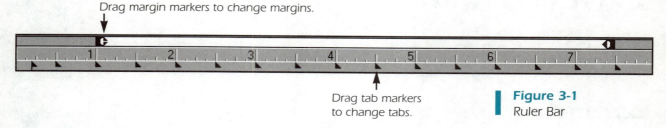

Figure 3-1
Ruler Bar

CHANGING THE MARGINS

The left and right margins in WordPerfect 6.0 for Windows are preset to one inch from the left and right edges of the page. The Ruler Bar makes it easy to change margins by using the mouse to click and drag the arrows to their new positions on the Ruler Bar. Margins can, however, be set more precisely through the dialog box.

Practice setting margins using the Ruler Bar:

▶ **EXERCISE 3-1**

1. Open the file named **basic.wpd** and display the Ruler Bar. Notice the margins are set at 1" and 7 1/2".
2. Move to the beginning of the document.
3. Position your mouse pointer on the left margin arrow.
4. Click and drag the arrow to its new position at **1 1/2"** on the Ruler Bar. As you do so, a vertical dashed line is displayed from the icon down to the bottom of the document window. You can repeat the process to move the right margin marker to its new position at **7"** on the Ruler Bar.
5. Close this file without saving it.

After you move the margin icons, the text in the document is immediately reformatted to reflect the new margin settings on the Ruler Bar.

WP40   **LESSON 3**   FORMATTING DOCUMENTS

Practice setting margins using the Margins dialog box:

> **EXERCISE 3-2**

   1. Open the file named **less1.wpd**.

2. Place the Insertion Point at the beginning of the second paragraph.

3. Choose <u>L</u>ayout and then <u>M</u>argins. The Margins dialog box (See Figure 3-2.) will appear and you can key the margins you wish to use; in this case, key `1.5` in the left margin box.

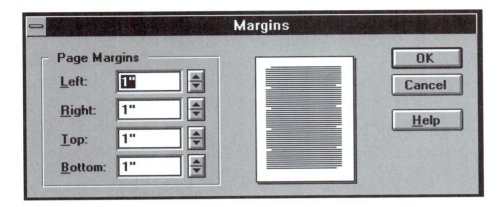

Figure 3-2
Margins dialog box

4. Press **Tab** and you will move automatically to the next box. Key `1.5` for the right margin. Note that you can change top and bottom margins by this method also; in this case, key `1.5` for the top margin and `1.5` for the bottom margin. You will see your changes reflected on the small page at the right of the dialog box. Then click on OK. Notice that the margin changes have taken effect.

5. Close the file without saving it.

If you double-click on the Ruler Bar on either of the margin markers, WordPerfect will open the Margins dialog box. If you click on the right mouse button with the mouse pointer in the margins area, WordPerfect will provide the QuickMenu shown in Figure 3-3.

Figure 3-3
QuickMenu-Margins

SETTING TABS

When you press Tab, the Insertion Point moves to an exact preset position. In WordPerfect, you do not need to set tabs unless you want to change the current tab settings. The default tab settings are left aligned at one-half inch intervals beginning at the left margin.

When you press Tab, the Insertion Point and the text on a line will move to the next tab setting. When you press Shift+Tab, the Insertion Point will move back to the previous setting.

Tabs can be set with the Ruler Bar or through the dialog box. The Ruler Bar provides an easier and more visual way of setting and changing tabs. Setting or changing tabs through the dialog box allows you to set your tabs more precisely.

SETTING TABS THROUGH THE RULER BAR

▶ **EXERCISE 3-3**

1. Be sure you have a blank screen.
2. Place the Insertion Point at the location where you want the new tab settings to begin, so the tab settings will take effect from that point on; in this case, at the beginning of the document. Now display the Ruler Bar. Notice the black triangles along the bottom of the Ruler Bar where the tabs are presently set.
3. Place the Insertion Point on one of the black triangles and click the right mouse button; then click on Clear All Tabs.
4. Set new tabs by clicking on the Ruler Bar where you want a new tab; in this case, on **2 1/4, 3 1/2, 4 3/4,** and **6.** Note that a vertical dashed line (Ruler Guide) will appear to help you see where the new tab setting will be placed in relation to the text.
5. Key the exercise in Figure 3-4. Begin at the left margin and use **Tab** to move from column to column. Press **Enter** at the end of each line.
6. Save the file with the name **food1** and close the file.

corn	eggs	juice	peas	lettuce
bread	cabbage	apple	macaroni	jam
milk	beans	cheese	oranges	butter

▍ Figure 3-4

The type of Tab code that WordPerfect inserts into your document when you press Tab is determined by the current tab setting. Four types of tab settings are available:

Left tab **[Tab]** (the default): When you press Tab to move to a left-aligned tab, the text you key is inserted to the right of the tab stop.

Center tab **[Cntr Tab]**: When you press Tab to move to a center-aligned tab, the text you key is centered over the tab stop.

Right tab **[Rgt Tab]**: When you press Tab to move to a right-aligned tab, the text you key is inserted to the left of the tab stop.

Decimal tab **[Dec Tab]**: When you press Tab to move to a decimal-aligned tab, text is inserted to the left of the tab until the align character (usually a period) is keyed. The text is then inserted to the right of the tab. This is especially useful for lining up columns of numbers and dollars and cents.

You can also select each of these same tab types with dot leaders. When you insert a Dot Leader tab, a row of dots is inserted in your text when you press Tab. Dot leaders are inserted from the Insertion Point to the next tab setting. Figure 3-5 shows how all kinds of tabs, including dot leaders, can be used.

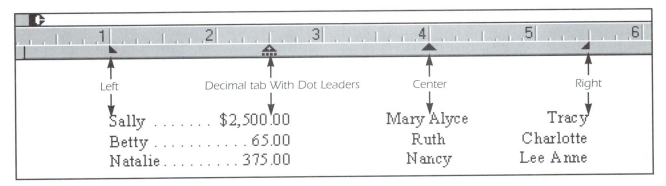

Figure 3-5
Tab examples

SETTING TABS THROUGH THE DIALOG BOX

By using the Tab Set dialog box, shown in Figure 3-6, you can set your tabs more precisely and make choices quickly. The Tab Set dialog box displays the type and position of the current settings in your document.

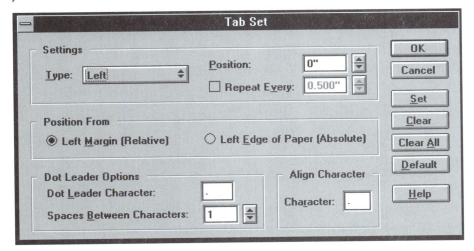

Figure 3-6
Tab Set dialog box

The Position From box lets you choose whether to make your tabs Absolute from the Left Edge of the Paper or Relative to the Left Margin. WordPerfect defaults to **Relative tabs.** This means that the dimensions you enter are relative to the left margin. If the margin changes, so does the actual tab stop.

Absolute tabs never change as the margin changes. They are always measured from the left edge of the page. When you set a tab at two inches, it is always two inches from the left edge of the page, regardless of the current margin. Whether you choose Left Edge of Paper or Left Margin, the choice affects all tab settings in the list—not just the current one.

DELETING AND CREATING NEW TABS

You can clear any or all of these tab settings, and you can change their type and position by following the steps below:

1. To delete a tab setting, drag it off the Ruler Bar with the mouse *or* key the tab to be deleted in the Position text box on the Tab Set dialog box, and then choose Clear. To delete *all* tabs quickly, choose Clear All at the right side of the dialog box.

2. To create a new tab setting, click on the Ruler Bar where you want the tab to occur *or* in the dialog box, key a new tab position number in the Position text box, choose the type of tab from the Type box, and click on Set. You must be sure to choose Set to define a new tab setting, and then choose OK.

Setting evenly spaced tabs with a specific interval between tabs is easier through the dialog box than through the Ruler Bar. To do so, check the Repeat Every text box on the Tab Set dialog box. The Position text box indicates the position for the first tab and the Repeat Every text box indicates the amount of space between each tab setting.

Practice setting tabs through the Tab Set dialog box:

▶ **EXERCISE 3-4**

1. Normally, you must be sure the Insertion Point is at the location where you want the new tab settings to begin, so the tab settings will take effect from that point on. In this case, since you are starting with a blank screen, the Insertion Point is at the beginning of the document.

2. Choose Layout, Line, and Tab Set, and the Tab Set dialog box will appear.

3. Choose the Clear All button at the right of the screen.

4. The next step is to choose the type of tab you want to set. In this case, you can leave the type at Left.

5. Move the Insertion Point to the Position text box, key 1.25, and then choose Set. You can key either decimals or fractions. After specifying the beginning tab setting in the Position text box, click on the Repeat Every text box and specify the distance between tabs. In this case, move the Insertion Point to the box and key 1 1/4 or 1.25.

6. Click on OK.

WP44 **LESSON 3** FORMATTING DOCUMENTS

7. Again key the exercise in Figure 3-4. Begin at the left margin and use **Tab** to move from column to column.

8. Save the file with the name **food2** and Close the file.

After keying your tabulated information, you will frequently want to return to the default settings. The Tab Set dialog box, not the Ruler Bar, is the easiest way to accomplish this. When you choose Default at the right side of the dialog box, WordPerfect resets the tab settings to left-aligned tabs every one-half inch.

Now perform the following exercise, applying more of what you have learned about tab setting.

▶ **EXERCISE 3-5**

Set the following tabs through the dialog box for the exercise illustrated in Figure 3-7. The first column is to be keyed at the left margin. Clear all tabs before you begin.

1. Set a Dot Decimal tab at **2.0** so that the second column will begin two inches from the left margin.
2. Set a Left tab at **3.0** for the third column.
3. Set another Dot Decimal tab at **5.0** for the fourth column.
4. Key the exercise, using **Tab** to move from column to column. Save the exercise with the name **pay.due,** and then Print a copy and Close the file.

```
Sally  . . .$450.00    Ross  . . . $55.55
Mary   . . .  36.50    Joe   . . . 325.00
Bill   . . . 127.50    Maria . . .   9.75
```

▎Figure 3-7

INDENTING TEXT

Using the Indent options is different from using Tab. When you use Tab, only the first line of a paragraph is indented. You use the Indent feature to move a complete paragraph one tab stop to the right until you press Enter.

You can indent in three ways:

1. *Indent* from the left margin only.
2. *Hanging Indent,* leaving the first line of the paragraph at the left margin and indenting the following lines.
3. *Double Indent* from both the right and left margins.

INDENT

To indent text on the left only:

- Click on the Indent icon on the Button Bar, *or*
- Choose Layout, Paragraph, and Indent.

An Indent code is placed in your document. Key the text you want indented. When you press Enter, the indent is completed.

The Indent code is useful when you wish to key a list of numbered items and you want the text to line up similar to the objectives at the beginning of this lesson.

HANGING INDENT

To leave the first line of a paragraph at the margin and indent the rest of the paragraph, follow these steps:

- Choose Layout, Paragraph, and Hanging Indent.

When you key the text and press Enter, the first line remains at the left margin and subsequent lines are indented.

DOUBLE INDENT

To indent text on the left and right, follow these steps:

- Choose Layout, Paragraph, and Double Indent.

The code is embedded in your text. Key the text which will be aligned an equal distance from the left and right margins. When you press Enter, the double indent is completed.

Double indent is particularly useful when you have to indent a quotation longer than three lines from both the left and right margins.

INDENTING EXISTING TEXT

You can apply all the Indent options to existing text. Just insert the Indent code(s) where you want the text to be indented.

> **EXERCISE 3-6**

1. Open the file you saved as **less1**.
2. Move the Insertion Point to the beginning of the first paragraph and click on the Indent icon on the Button Bar, OR choose Layout, Paragraph, and Indent.
3. Move the Insertion Point to the beginning of the second paragraph and choose Layout, Paragraph, and Hanging Indent.

4. Move the Insertion Point to the beginning of the third paragraph and choose Layout, Paragraph, and Double Indent.
5. Save this file as **less3,** but do not Close it.

VIEW

You can work with your documents in three different modes or views: **Draft, Page, and Two Page.** You access each of these through the View pull-down menu.

Draft view in WordPerfect 6.0 for Windows is near **WYSIWYG** (What You See Is What You Get). When you key, WordPerfect attempts to use fonts in the document window that match the fonts used by your printer. Italic, bold, and underline appear as italic, bold, and underline. You can usually work faster in Draft view because certain formatting features, such as headers and footers, do not appear. As a result, information displays more quickly as you move through your document.

Page view is a full WYSIWYG environment. In addition to matching fonts and appearance features, a document is formatted as it will look when it is printed, including headers, footers, footnotes, and endnotes.

Two-Page view is similar to Page view, except that two consecutive pages are displayed side by side in the same document window.

PAGE BREAKS

When text reaches the bottom margin of a page, WordPerfect automatically inserts a soft page break to indicate that you have filled one page and you are starting another. The page break is described as soft because its location is likely to change as you edit your document. When you add or delete any content, WordPerfect reformats the document and will place the soft page breaks in new locations as needed.

HARD PAGE BREAKS

You can insert a hard page break anywhere you want to force a new page to begin. Even though you may later insert text before the page break, the page break will always begin a new page. In Page view, a hard page break looks the same as a soft page break. In Draft view, a soft page break is represented by a single line extending across the document window. A hard page break is represented by a double line extending across the document window.

To insert a hard page break, place the Insertion Point where you want to end the page, and then:

- Choose Insert and then Page Break, *or* press **Ctrl+Enter**.

EXERCISE 3-7

1. Change to **Draft** view.
2. Insert a hard page break after the third paragraph. Notice the double line for the hard page break.
3. Then change to **Page** view and notice that the double line is no longer there and the page break looks like any other page break.
4. Save the file as **less4** and Close the file.

EXERCISE 3-8

1. Key the material shown in Figure 3-8.
2. Double indent the second paragraph.
3. Save this document with the name **quote**. Do NOT Print a copy. Close the file.

```
The Secretary's Commission on Achieving Necessary
Skills (SCANS) spent 12 months talking to business
owners, to public employers, to the people who
manage employees daily, to union officials, and to
workers on the line and at their desks.  Commission
members talked to them in their stores, shops,
government offices, and manufacturing facilities.
Their message was the same across the country and
in every kind of job:
     Good jobs depend on people who can put
     knowledge to work.  New workers must
     be creative and responsible problem
     solvers and have the skills and attitudes
     on which employers can build.  Traditional
     jobs are changing and new jobs are
     created every day.  High- paying but
     unskilled jobs are disappearing.  Employers
     and employees share the belief that all
     workplaces must "work smarter."
```

Figure 3-8

CHANGING JUSTIFICATION

WordPerfect 6.0 for Windows offers you several options for how the margins will be justified.

Selecting **Left justification** will cause the text to be aligned at the left margin. Selecting **Right justification** will cause each line to be aligned at the right. Selecting **Center justification** will center each line until you select a different Justification option. When you create documents with **Full justification**, WordPerfect will adjust the amount of space between the words and letters so the text will be aligned on both the left and right sides of the document. Selecting **All justification** (usually for a title or a heading) will evenly space between the left and right margins. This feature is helpful if you are keying a title for a publication such as a newsletter.

- Position the Insertion Point where you want to change the justification.
- Click on the Justification icon on the Power Bar. Drag the selection bar to your new justification setting and release the mouse button, *or*
- Choose Layout and then Justification, and highlight your new justification setting and release the mouse button.

CHANGING LINE SPACING

As you create a document, lines are automatically single-spaced, with no extra space between them. By clicking on the 1.0 (or single spacing) button on the Power Bar, you can change to 1.5, 2.0, or Other spacing. If you select Other, the Line Spacing dialog box will appear and you can key any amount that you desire.

You can also access the Line Spacing dialog box by choosing Layout, Line, and Spacing.

▶ **EXERCISE 3-9**

Open the file named **basic** and be sure the Insertion Point is at the beginning of the document. Make the following changes using the Ruler and Power bars:

1. Click and drag the left margin on the Ruler Bar to **1.5"** and the right margin to **7"**.
2. Position the mouse pointer on the Ruler Bar on the tab located at the 2-inch marker. Click and drag the marker to **1.75"**.
3. Position the Insertion Point at the beginning of the second paragraph, and then click on the Justification icon on the Power Bar and choose Center.
4. Move the Insertion Point to the beginning of the third paragraph and select Left justification.
5. Click on the Line Spacing icon on the Power Bar and change to Double Spacing.
6. Save this document as **basic.rul.**
7. Print a copy and Close the file.

In Lesson 1, you saved a document called **less1**. Open that file now and be sure the Insertion Point is at the beginning of the document. Make the following changes, using menus and dialog boxes rather than the Ruler and Power bars:

1. Change the margins to **.75"** for both left and right margins.
2. Change the line spacing to **1.5.**
3. Clear all tabs and then set a Left tab at **1".**
4. Save this document as **less1.alt** and Print one copy. Close the document.

REVIEW

TRUE/FALSE

Circle the correct answer.

1. T F The Ruler Bar provides a quick and easy way to set margins and line spacing.
2. T F The Ruler Bar provides an easier and more visual way of setting and hanging tabs.
3. T F When you use a Left tab, the text you key is inserted to the left of the tab stop.
4. T F Absolute tabs are always measured from the left edge of the page.
5. T F When in the Tab Set dialog box, be sure to choose Set to define a new tab setting.
6. T F When text reaches the bottom of the page, WordPerfect automatically inserts a hard page break.
7. T F When you create documents with Full justification, the amount of space between words and letters will be aligned on both the left and right sides of the document.

COMPLETION

Fill in the blank.

1. Setting or changing tabs or margins through the _____ _____ allows you to set them more precisely.
2. A _____ _____ is especially useful for lining up columns of numbers.
3. When you insert a _____ _____ tab, a row of dots is inserted in your text when you press Tab.
4. WordPerfect defaults to Relative tabs, which means that the dimensions you enter are relative to the _____ _____.
5. You can usually work faster in _____ view.
6. Use _____ to move a complete paragraph one tab stop to the right.

LESSON 3 FORMATTING DOCUMENTS WP51

Reference Question: Go to the WordPerfect 6.0 for Windows documentation Glossary and find the definitions for Codes, Default, Deselect, Insertion Point, Mouse Pointer, and the two definitions of Select. Write them below.

REVIEW EXERCISES

Key the document shown in Figure 3-9, using single spacing and pressing **Enter** only at the ends of paragraphs and to leave blank lines. Do NOT double space between paragraphs or side headings. Save the document with the name **recycle**. Go to the beginning of the document and do the following:

1. Center the title and double space the text after it.
2. Change the left margin to **1.5"** and the right margin to **7.75"** (if you are using the Ruler Bar) or **.75"** (if you are using the dialog box).
3. Indent the first line of each paragraph using the default tabs.
4. Put the side headings (Paper, Glass, Cans & Metal, and Plastics) on a line by themselves.
5. Proofread the copy carefully.
6. Save it on your disk with the name **recycle1**. Do not close the file.

```
RECYCLE BEGINNING TODAY!
Whether you visit an attended drop-off location or you
participate in a pilot curbside route, you may now
recycle most of your household waste with your local
Sanitation District.  Simply provide clean materials
sorted according to the categories listed on this
convenient guide.
Paper
Your waste paper is valuable material because it can
be manufactured into fiberboard packaging. Nearly all
your paper is acceptable and it is not necessary to
sort it.  Newspaper, stationery, corrugated boxes,
magazines, and telephone books are most common.
Please remember that all paper must be free of
plastics, metal fasteners, or any other contaminants.
Milk cartons and tissue paper cannot be recycled.
Please prepare your paper materials by placing them in
a paper sack or tying them with twine of natural fiber.
Glass
Your glass containers can be remanufactured into new
glass containers found in most kitchens. Take a moment
to remove labels by soaking in used dishwater.  Lids
and rings must be removed. Please rinse and separate
by color.
CLEAR--Purely clear glass only.
AMBER--All shades of brown and yellow.
GREEN--All shades of green and shades of blue.
Only food and beverage containers made of glass are
acceptable.  Ceramics, glass cookware, tableware, and
```

```
plate glass are not acceptable since they have a
different melting temperature in a glass furnace.
Cans & Metal
Your household cans and metals can be processed and
marketed as valuable raw material.  Please rinse,
remove labels, and separate into these categories:
Beverage Cans:  Soft drink style only.
Steel Cans:  Food cans and some drink cans.
Household Aluminum:  Foil wrap and frozen food
containers.
Plastics
Most household products packaged in plastic will bear
one of these six codes with a recycle symbol on the
bottom.  Bottles for milk, soft drinks, and detergents
are the most common. Check most of your plastics and
polystyrene (today's styrofoam), and you will find that
it can be recycled.  Remove lids and rings.  Please
rinse and sort.
```

Figure 3-9

▶ **REVIEW EXERCISE 3-2**

Make the following changes to the current document, using whichever of the methods presented in this lesson you believe will be most effective for you.

1. Keep the left margin of 1.5", and change the right margin to **7.5"** (on the Ruler Bar) or **1"** (on the dialog box).

2. Press **Enter** three times to add another inch to the top margin above the title.

3. Center the group of lines beginning with CLEAR, AMBER, and GLASS and the group of lines beginning with Beverage Cans, Steel Cans, and Household Aluminum.

4. Print one copy and save this document as **recycle2.**

5. Close the file.

LESSON 4

Reveal Codes, Speller, and Envelope

OBJECTIVES

Upon completion of this lesson, you will be able to:

1. Use Reveal Codes and adjust the size of the Reveal Codes display.
2. Delete codes.
3. Troubleshoot with Reveal Codes.
4. Use the Speller to check your documents.
5. Understand how QuickCorrect operates.
6. Prepare single envelopes.

REVEAL CODES

WordPerfect inserts a hidden code for almost every feature you use in a document. These codes are very important since they determine how your document will look on the screen and how it is printed. Usually you do not see these codes. Sometimes, however, you do need to see the codes to be sure they are placed where you want them or to help you in editing a document.

When you use Reveal Codes, the document window is split into two sections. The top section of the window shows the document as it was keyed. The bottom section of the window shows the same portion of the document with the codes displayed where they were inserted. (See Figure 4-1 on the next page.)

WP55

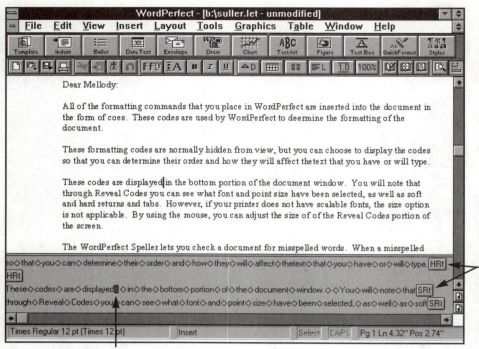

Figure 4-1
Reveal Codes screen

To see the codes inserted by WordPerfect:

1. Open the document named **recycle2.**

2. After the document appears on the screen, choose <u>V</u>iew and then Reveal <u>C</u>odes, <u>OR</u> press **Alt+F3.**

3. Press the up and down arrow keys several times to find your Insertion Point in both the top part of the screen and in the bottom part of the screen.

4. Move through the document and see the **[SRt]** (soft return) codes at the end of those lines which auto wrapped to the next line and the **[HRt]** (hard return) codes where you pressed Enter.

5. Note the **[Left Tab]** codes at the beginning of the paragraphs. Press **PgUp** and note also at the beginning of the document how your line spacing and left/right margins are shown in Reveal Codes.

6. Note the **[Just]** code to center justify the list after the third paragraph. This is an example of an expandable code. When you place the Insertion Point immediately before the code or place the mouse pointer on the code and click with the left mouse button, the code will expand. Do this now to show **[Just Center].**

7. Close the Reveal Codes window by choosing <u>V</u>iew and Reveal <u>C</u>odes again <u>OR</u> by pressing **Alt+F3** again.

▶ **EXERCISE 4-1**

ADJUSTING THE SIZE OF THE REVEAL CODES SCREEN

To adjust the size of the Reveal Codes screen, move the mouse pointer onto the dividing line between the screens until the mouse pointer changes to a double-headed arrow, and drag the line upward or downward. You can also turn off Reveal Codes by dragging the line to either the very top or the very bottom of the screen and releasing the mouse button.

As you learn more WordPerfect features, you will learn about the codes that are inserted into the document. Some codes, such as **[SRt]**, are inserted automatically by WordPerfect, but most codes are inserted by the person who is keying or formatting the document. For example, if you underline a word, the code **[Und]** is inserted at the beginning of the word and **[Und]** is inserted at the end of the word.

Some codes are single codes while others, such as Bold and Underline, come in pairs.

DELETING CODES

You cannot see to delete codes except in Reveal Codes. You can delete most codes the same way you delete characters. Use Backspace to delete to the left of the Insertion Point or use Delete to delete to the right of the Insertion Point in Reveal Codes. You can also delete a code by clicking and dragging the code off the screen.

TROUBLESHOOTING WITH REVEAL CODES

You will find Reveal Codes to be an invaluable feature to keep you informed about what is really happening in WordPerfect and to help you troubleshoot when you have problems. Sometimes a stray code or wrong code is inserted accidentally when you mistakenly press a key or command. These codes can cause some strange things to happen; for example, a misplaced Hard Page code could cause a new page. Without Reveal Codes, the problems would be almost impossible to find and cure. With Reveal Codes, the problems are easy to solve.

Whenever WordPerfect does not perform as you think it should, go into Reveal Codes where you can see the specific location and type of codes that WordPerfect is using to format your document.

When you want to edit some text, but you do not want to accidentally change or delete the codes, go into Reveal Codes so that you can see where you are deleting and adding. In fact, some people make a habit of performing all heavy editing tasks while in Reveal Codes.

YOU SHOULD GET IN THE HABIT OF USING REVEAL CODES TO HELP YOU MAKE YOUR OWN TASKS EASIER!

▶ **EXERCISE 4-2**

1. Close any documents on your screen. Start a new document by inserting the date code, which you learned about in Lesson 1, to obtain the current date.

2. Key the document shown in Figure 4-2 exactly as it appears. Do not bold the words in bold, but key the errors in the words exactly as they are shown. Do <u>NOT</u> correct errors! Press **Enter** only at the ends of paragraphs or short lines and to leave blank lines.

3. Save this document with the name **suller.let.**

Insert Date Code

(Insert 3 blank lines)

Miss Mellody Suller
4305 University Avenue
Indianapolis, IN 46250

Dear Mellody:

All the formatting commands that you place in WordPerfect are inserted into the document in the form of **coes**. These codes are used by WordPerfect to **deermine** the formatting of the document.

These formatting codes are normally hidden from view, but you can choose to display the codes so that you can determine their order and how they will affect **thetext** that you have or will type.

These codes are displayed in the bottom portion of the document window. You will note that through Reveal Codes you can see what font and point size have been selected, as well as soft and hard returns and tabs. However, if your printer does not have scalable fonts, the size option is not applicable. By using the mouse, you can adjust the size **of of** the Reveal Codes portion of the screen.

The WordPerfect Speller lets you check a document for misspelled words. When a **mispelled** word is found, the Speller gives you several possible spelling solutions so you can easily replace your mistake. The Speller is a very powerful feature, but it isn't omnipotent.

```
You have to have a general idea of the word you're
trying to spell, and you cannot avoid the problem of
words that our spelled correctly but aren't the words
you want. WordPerfect checks to see if the word on the
screen is a correctly spelled word, not necessarily
the correct word for the occassion.

Sincerely yours,

(Insert 3 blank lines)

Kathleen P. Wagoner

yrs
```

Figure 4-2

CHECKING YOUR SPELLING

Before printing any document, you should first check your spelling. WordPerfect provides a dictionary containing approximately 115,000 words that makes it extremely quick and easy to check for spelling or keying errors. You can add other words to the dictionary, but you must make sure that any words you add are spelled correctly. You don't want to add misspelled words to the Speller's dictionary.

Spell-check the document you've named **suller.let** by following the instructions below VERY CAREFULLY. The instructions assume that you keyed the misspelled words as they appear in Figure 4-2. Most other typographical errors that you might have made as you keyed the letter will also be caught, so you may find extra steps to be performed in the process.

▶ **EXERCISE 4-3**

You can begin the spell-check with either of the following methods:

- Click on the Speller icon on the Power Bar, OR
- Choose Tools, and then Speller. The dialog box shown in Figure 4-3 will appear.

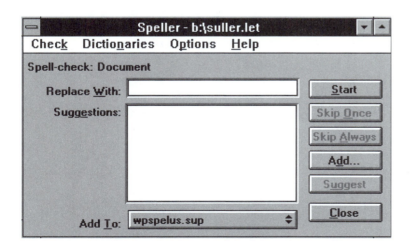

Figure 4-3
Speller dialog box

1. Choose S̲tart to begin spell-checking. As the spelling is checked, WordPerfect highlights each word that it thinks is misspelled and displays the dialog box shown in Figure 4-4.

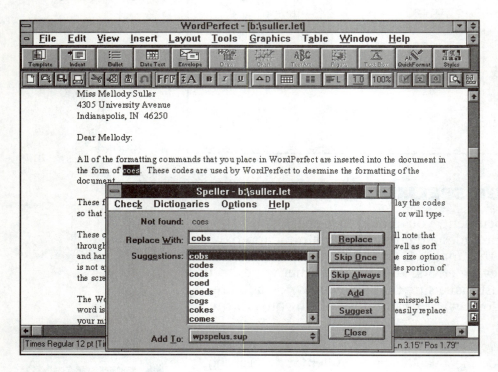

Figure 4-4
Choices shown to replace `coes`.

2. The first word that should be highlighted in the letter and in the dialog box should be `Mellody`. Since this is a person's name, you should check the spelling carefully, move to the Skip O̲nce button, and click. Do the same on `Suller` and any other proper names.

3. The next word that should be highlighted in the letter and in the dialog box (provided you did not make other errors) should be `coes`. WordPerfect displays several possible replacement spellings, as shown in Figure 4-4. The correct word may or may not be among these words. But in this case, the correct word, `codes`, is displayed.

4. Select the word `codes` by double-clicking on it or by moving the selection bar to it and choosing R̲eplace. The word `coes` is now replaced by `codes` and the spell-checking continues. Follow the same process to correct `deermine`.

5. To correct a misspelled word yourself (if none of the suggestions are correct), move the mouse pointer to the highlighted error in the body of the text and use editing keys such as **Backspace** and **Delete** to correct the word. A common mistake is to leave out a space between two words. To make the correction, you can add a space to correct `the text`, and then choose R̲esume.

6. WordPerfect also checks for double words (a common keying error). Click on Replace to replace the duplicate words with a single word.

7. Continue spell-checking this document. The next words that should be highlighted in the letter and in the dialog box (provided you did not make other errors) should be mispelled and occassion. You should know how to handle these.

8. Note that our was not highlighted because it is a word that is spelled correctly—ALTHOUGH IT IS NOT THE RIGHT WORD FOR THAT SPOT IN THE TEXT. As explained earlier, WordPerfect will not catch everything. Did you notice that the word should be "are" rather than "our"?

9. When spell-checking is finished, a dialog box appears to let you know. Choose Yes to close the Speller window.

10. Save the document as **suller1.let**. Print a copy of the document and Close the file.

You must save your document after you have spell-checked it. If you don't, all your changes will be lost.

If you want the Speller to check a paragraph you have just keyed, just Select or highlight the paragraph (remember, an easy way to do that is by quickly clicking your mouse four times on the paragraph) and then open Speller.

You can exit from the Speller before it has finished by choosing Close in the Speller window. Then Save your document so the spelling corrections made up to that point won't be lost.

QUICKCORRECT

Beginning with WordPerfect 6.0a for Windows, you will find QuickCorrect in Tools. This feature automatically replaces errors in some of the commonly miskeyed or misspelled words. For instance, if you accidentally key "adn," it is automatically replaced with "and" as soon as you press the Space Bar or another word delimiter (comma, period, semicolon, etc.).

Choose Tools and then QuickCorrect, and the QuickCorrect dialog box shown in Figure 4-5 on the next page will appear. WordPerfect provides a list of some commonly misspelled, miskeyed, or abbreviated words. You can also add your own words by keying your words in the Replace and With boxes. Notice also that you have the choice of whether to Replace Errors As You Type and Correct Initial Double Uppercase (THe). For more information on QuickCorrect, see your User's Guide.

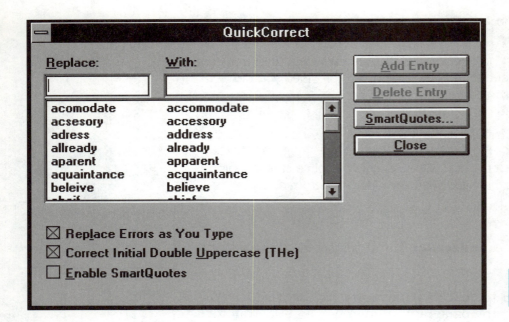

Figure 4-5
QuickCorrect dialog box

▶ **EXERCISE 4-4**

1. Now open the document named **devices1** which you keyed earlier with some errors in it. Spell-check this document and proofread it for those errors which WordPerfect does not catch. Save this document as **devices3**. Print a copy.

2. Open the QuickCorrect dialog box and look at the list of words. Be sure that you will have your documents corrected as you key and that double uppercase letters will also be corrected. Close the file.

ENVELOPES

One of the great features of WordPerfect is how they have made it possible for you to create an envelope very quickly and easily. You can create envelopes to go with an existing document, such as a letter, or you can create single envelopes as you need them.

Before beginning the following exercises, be sure to check with your instructor to determine if and where you are to print these envelopes in your classroom or laboratory.

In the following exercise, you will learn how to create an envelope for an existing letter. Once you have learned how, you can easily prepare an envelope as you write a letter.

WP62   **LESSON 4**   REVEAL CODES, SPELLER, AND ENVELOPE

 1. Open the file named **suller.let**.

2. Choose <u>L</u>ayout and then En<u>v</u>elope, or click on the Envelope icon on the Button Bar. The Envelope dialog box shown in Figure 4-6 will appear. WordPerfect displays the last return address used to create an envelope, or you can easily key the return address you desire. When WordPerfect finds a mailing address in the current document, it is retrieved into the mailing address window. (In order to be retrieved, a mailing address must be followed by two hard returns in your document.)

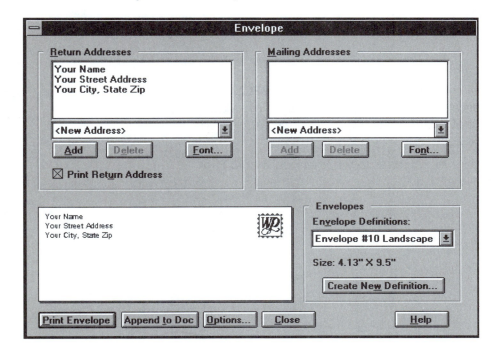

Figure 4-6
Envelope dialog box

3. Key your own return address. Make sure Print Return Address is selected.

4. The mailing address should already have been inserted.

5. Any printer that prints graphically can add the USPS POSTNET Bar Code to your envelope. To include the Bar Code, choose <u>O</u>ptions. You can select either Include and Position Above Address <u>OR</u> Include and Position Below Address, and then choose OK. In this case, choose Below. The Envelope dialog box provides you with a preview of how the envelope appears and how it should print.

6. Follow the directions of your instructor to choose <u>P</u>rint Envelope to print the envelope without inserting it into your document, or choose Append <u>t</u>o Doc to insert the envelope at the end of your document where you can Print <u>OR</u> Save it.

7. Close the file.

In the following exercise, you will learn how to create a single envelope without first creating a letter.

1. Choose Layout and then Envelope, or click on the Envelope icon on the Button Bar. The Envelope dialog box will appear.

2. WordPerfect will display the last return address used to create an envelope, which in this case should be your own return address which you used in Exercise 4-5. If for any reason, your address is not in the Return Address box, key it now.

3. Move the Insertion Point to the Mailing Address box and key the following mailing address:

    South-Western Publishing Co.
    5101 Madison Road
    Cincinnati, OH 45227

    Because you have already chosen in Exercise 4-5 to use the POSTNET Bar Code, it may automatically appear with your address in the Mailing Address box and on the preview of the envelope. If it doesn't, click on the box at the right of the POSTNET Bar Code.

4. Follow the directions of your instructor as to whether you should Print this envelope. Close the file.

▶ **EXERCISE 4-6**

REVIEW

TRUE/FALSE

Circle the correct answer.

1. T F When you use Reveal Codes, the document window is split into two sections.
2. T F A Soft Return code is shown at the end of those lines which auto wrapped to the next line.
3. T F All codes are inserted by the person who is keying or formatting the document.
4. T F The [SRt] code is inserted automatically by WordPerfect.
5. T F QuickCorrect will automatically correct some commonly misspelled, miskeyed, or abbreviated words.
6. T F WordPerfect automatically puts the USPS POSTNET Bar Code on every envelope prepared in WordPerfect.

COMPLETION

Fill in the blank.

1. _____ determine how your document will look on the screen and how it is printed.
2. When you use _____ _____, the bottom section of the window displays the document showing where the codes are inserted.
3. A _____ _____ code is shown at the end of those lines where you pressed Enter.
4. To delete a code to the right of the Insertion Point in Reveal Codes, use _____.
5. You can _____ words to the dictionary if they do not appear in the dictionary.
6. You must _____ your document after you have spell-checked. If you don't, all your changes will be lost.

Reference Question: Look in the Appendix of the Reference Manual or User's Guide to find Troubleshooting. Find the Cause and Solution for the following Problem and write them below.

When I insert a code, the code is not inserted at the Insertion Point.

LESSON 5

Enhancing Text Appearance

OBJECTIVES

Upon completion of this lesson, you will be able to:

1. Change the font typeface, font size, and font style.
2. Make changes in appearance (bold, italic, underline), position, and relative size.
3. Make changes after keying.
4. Center text horizontally and vertically between margins on a page.
5. Align text at the right margin (Flush Right).
6. Convert already keyed text to lowercase, uppercase, or initial capitals.

WordPerfect 6.0 for Windows offers a variety of features on the Power Bar and through the Layout menu that will help you to enhance the appearance of the text.

FONTS

Changing fonts can bring about very dramatic differences in the appearance of the text and definitely enhance the message the document conveys. A **font** is a set of characters with a specific design or typeface. The fonts available to you will depend upon the printer you are using and on what TrueType fonts have been installed in your version of Windows. WordPerfect 6.0 for Windows is designed to work with three elements of fonts: the font face (such as Times Roman or Courier), the font style, (such as Bold or Italic), and the font size (10, 12, 14, etc.).

The first step is always to position the Insertion Point where you want the change to occur.

The quickest way to *see* what font typefaces are available to you and to change fonts is to click on the Font button on the Power Bar. A drop-down menu listing all fonts available will appear. (Beginning with WordPerfect 6.0a for Windows, the last four fonts used are displayed at the top of this drop-down font list.) To select a specific font, click on the name of the font you want. Those fonts which are available to you through your printer have a small printer before the name of the font. All the TrueType fonts have two T's before the name of the font.

The quickest way to *choose* the size font you want is to click on the Font Size button on the Power Bar. You are provided a list of sizes from 6 to 48 from which to select. Font sizes are measured in points (72 points to an inch). The larger the number, the larger the font size will be. Click on the size of the font you desire.

BOLD, ITALIC, AND UNDERLINE

The quickest way to *choose* an appearance you want is to click on the appearance buttons on the Power Bar. These are:

B for Bold

I for Italic

U for Underline

You can also bold text by keying **Crtl+B**, then keying the text you want to be in bold, and then keying **Ctrl+B** again. You can also italicize text by keying **Ctrl+I**, keying the text you want italicized, and then keying **Ctrl+I** again. And you can underline text by keying **Ctrl+U**, keying the text you want underlined, and then keying **Ctrl+U** again.

▶ **EXERCISE 5-1**

Take a few minutes and practice changing font faces and font sizes until you become comfortable with the process of changing these. Then key the following lines in the font face and size described:

```
This is 18 point Arial.
This is 10 point Century-WP.
This is 48 point Stencil-WP.
This is 36 point Commercial Script-WP.
```

Print a copy of these lines. Save the file as **fonts1** and Close the file.

CHANGING FONTS THROUGH THE DIALOG BOX

In some instances, you may want to open the Font dialog box shown in Figure 5-1 because you can change *all* of the various font options directly through this dialog box.

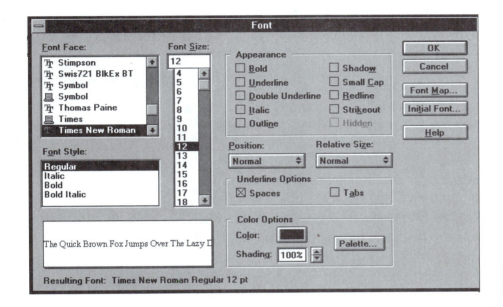

Figure 5-1
Font dialog box

- Choose Layout and then Font, *or* double-click on the Font button on the Power Bar.

At the left side of the screen, you can choose the Font Face, Font Size, and Font Style you want. You can see what your choices look like in the box in the lower left of the dialog box.

CHANGING APPEARANCE, POSITION, AND RELATIVE SIZE

On the right side of the Font dialog box, there is a list of text Appearance attributes which lets you change the appearance of the text by clicking on the box for the attribute you want.

If you click on the Position box, a pop-up list will appear from which you can change from Normal position which prints on the line, Superscript, which will print above the line, *or* to Subscript, which will print below the line. Superscript and Subscript are especially useful when you must key formulas (such as H_2O or $E=MC^2$).

If you click on the Relative Size box, you can choose from Fine, Small, Normal, Large, Very Large, or Extra Large type. The advantage of using Relative Size attributes is that if you change a font at the beginning of your document, the sizes will automatically adjust throughout the entire document.

MAKING CHANGES AFTER KEYING

If you have already keyed some text and then determine that you want to change the size and appearance, you can make changes afterwards. To make such changes, you must first Select (highlight) the block of text you want to change. Then choose the font, size, and appearance you want. The font change you make will then affect the Selected text only.

▶ **EXERCISE 5-2**

1. Access the Font dialog box.
2. Now take a few minutes and practice changing font faces, font sizes, and font styles until you become comfortable with the process of changing these through the dialog box. Change some of these before you key them and some after keying. Remember, you can see what the changes will look like if you watch the box in the lower left of the dialog box.
3. Practice changing the appearance of the font by changing some of the appearance attributes until you understand what is available and feel comfortable making the changes.
4. Practice using the Position box to key some text in both Subscript and Superscript.
5. Practice using the Relative Size box to become familiar with the relative size of a font when you choose Fine, Small, Large, Very Large, and Extra Large. Then return the size to Normal.
6. Now on a clear screen, key the following lines in the font face, size, and appearance described:

   ```
   This is 17 point Arial and Bold.
   This is 11 point Century-WP and Italic.
   This is 40 point Stencil-WP.
   This is 32 point Commercial Script-WP and
   Underline.
   ```

7. Print a copy of these lines. Save the file as **fonts2** and Close the file.

If you are making only a few changes, you may wish to use the buttons on the Power Bar; however, if you have a number of changes to make at one time, it is advantageous to work through the Font dialog box.

CENTERING

Text can be centered both horizontally and vertically on the page. The following sections explain how to center lines between the left and right margins and how to center a page of text between the top and bottom margins.

CENTERING ONE OR MORE LINES

Whenever you want to center one or more lines as you key them:

- Click on Layout, Line, and Center.

The Insertion Point moves to the center between the left and right margins.

When you choose the command to center a line, a **[Hd Center on Marg]** code is placed at the beginning of the line. The **[HRt]** at the end of the line turns off centering. A **[Tab]**, **[Hd Left Ind]**, or **[Flsh Rgt]** (Flush Right) code will also end centering. Look for these codes when you are in Reveal Codes.

Now perform Exercises 5-3 through 5-6 all as one document.

▶ **EXERCISE 5-3**

1. Center the following phrase: `WordPerfect for Windows`. The text is centered as you key it.
2. Press **Enter** to end centering and return to the left margin on the next line.

CENTERING TEXT THAT HAS ALREADY BEEN KEYED

To center a line of text that has already been keyed, move the Insertion Point to the beginning of the line and select the Center command.

▶ **EXERCISE 5-4**

1. Try this now by keying `MEMORANDUM` at the left margin.
2. Move back to the beginning of the line and choose Layout, Line, and then Center.
3. The word `MEMORANDUM` will be centered. Open Reveal Codes to see the codes that have been inserted.

CENTERING WITH JUSTIFICATION

Remember that justification can also be used to center text. This option is best for centering a group of lines. You can use the Center Justification option without having to choose the Center command before keying each line. You can also use this option to center text that has already been keyed.

You can use either the Justification button on the Power Bar, *or*

- Choose Layout, Justification, and Center.

CENTER PAGE

WordPerfect can center a page vertically between the top and bottom margins with a command known as Center.

- Click on Layout, Page, and Center Page.

A Center Page(s) dialog box will appear, offering a choice of centering the Current Page, Current and Subsequent Pages, or No Centering. Click on your choice, and then click on OK.

FLUSH RIGHT

To align a line of text at the right margin, use the Flush Right command. Flush Right can be used before or after the text has been entered. Right Justification should be used for aligning an entire section of text.

To place text ending at the right margin:

- Click on Layout, Line, and Flush Right.

The Insertion Point moves to the right margin. As you key the text, it moves left. Press **Enter** and the text aligns with the right margin.

> **EXERCISE 5-5**

1. Move the Insertion Point to the beginning of the line and choose the Flush Right command.
2. Key the current date. It will end at the right margin.

                                                      Current Date

> **EXERCISE 5-6**

1. Key the following at the left margin: Your Name
2. Now go back and insert the Flush Right command before Your Name. Your Name will end at the right margin. Close this document without saving it.

CONVERTING CASE (UPPERCASE/LOWERCASE)

You can use either the Shift key or the Caps Lock key to obtain a series of characters in uppercase. If you have already keyed text in lowercase and then you want to convert it to uppercase (*or* you want to convert uppercase to lowercase), *or* you want to change the text to Initial Capitals (first letter of each word capitalized), you can use the Select feature to highlight the text you want to change, and then choose Edit and Convert Case.

You will be able to make your documents much more attractive now that you know a number of different ways to format the text and how to easily change both the appearance and size of the text.

Key the document shown in Figure 5-2 just as it is shown. Save the document with the name **membcom.let.**

▶ **EXERCISE 5-7**

```
Current Date

(Leave 3 blank lines here)

Dear Member:

I hope you will be able to attend the membership
committee meeting scheduled for (insert a date two
weeks in the future).  We will be discussing these
questions:

1. When should we conduct the membership drive for
next year?

2. What date should we set for the next social?
Should it be before or after the annual membership
drive?

3. When should we send out the program material for
next year?  Should we send it to members only or
send the complete mailing to all prospective
members?

We have had a successful first year, but we must keep
up the momentum to assure that we increase our
membership and do not lose any of our current members.

Please plan now to attend this very important meeting.
If you are not able to attend, please let me know
your opinions on the above questions.  We want the
input of every member of the committee.

Sincerely,

(Leave 3 blank lines here)

Mary Doe, Chairperson
Membership Committee
```

▎Figure 5-2

Now revise the document as follows:

1. Move the current date so that it is aligned at the right margin (Flush Right).
2. Indent the numbered items so that all lines of text in these items begin at the same point.
3. Double indent the paragraph which begins We have had...

4. Delete the salutation and complimentary close. Move the printed signature lines

        Mary Doe, Chairperson
        Membership Committee

    so that they end at the right margin.

5. Center the entire document vertically on the page.

6. Save this document as **membcom.rev** and Print a copy. Look at the document with the codes revealed so that you will become thoroughly familiar with the types of codes used in this document. Close the file.

▶ **EXERCISE 5-8**

Now key the text of the document shown in Figure 5-3. Do NOT apply the attributes of underline, bold, and italic. You will format the document after you have keyed it. Save it with the name **wkplace.**

Workplace Know-How

All employees of the future should have a basic workplace know-how so that they can succeed in their jobs. The know-how identified by The Secretary's Commission on Achieving Necessary Skills (SCANS) is made up of five competencies and a three-part foundation of skills and personal qualities that are needed for solid job performance. These are:

<u>Workplace Competencies</u>

Effective workers can productively use:

Resources - They know how to allocate time, money, materials, space and staff.

Interpersonal Skills - They can acquire and evaluate data, organize and maintain files, interpret and communicate, and use computers to process information.

Systems - They understand social, organizational, and technological systems; they can monitor and correct performance; and they can design or improve systems.

Technology - They can select equipment and tools, apply technology to specific tasks, and maintain and troubleshoot equipment.

<u>Foundation Skills</u>

Competent workers in the high-performance workplace need:

Basic Skills - reading, writing, arithmetic and mathematics, speaking and listening.

Thinking Skills - the ability to learn, to reason, to think creatively, to make decisions, and to solve problems.

Personal Qualities - individual responsibility, self-esteem and self-management, sociability, and integrity.

Figure 5-3

Now revise this document as follows:

1. Center the title Workplace Know-How and change it to upper-case. Change the size to Very Large.
2. Underline Workplace Competencies and change to bold and uppercase.
3. Format the title of each of the competencies (Resources, Interpersonal Skills, Systems, and Technology) in bold and italic.
4. Underline Foundation Skills and change to bold and uppercase.
5. Format the title of each of the foundation skills (Basic Skills, Thinking Skills, and Personal Qualities) in bold and italics.
6. Format each of the workplace competencies and foundation skills in a hanging indent format.
7. Add your name after the document in Fine print.
8. Center the document vertically on the page.
9. Using Reveal Codes, look for the paired codes for bold, italic, and underline. Find the codes for hanging indent.
10. Save the document as **wkplace.rev** and Print a copy. Close the file.

REVIEW

TRUE/FALSE

Circle the correct answer.

1. T   F   Text can be aligned at the right margin with the Flush Right command.

2. T   F   When you use tabs to indent, each line will be indented until you press Enter.

3. T   F   Font sizes are measured in points.

4. T   F   Center justification should be used when you wish to center a group of lines.

5. T   F   To make size or appearance changes after keying, you must first use Select to highlight the block of text you want to change.

COMPLETION

Fill in the blank.

1. The fonts available to you through your printer have a small _____ pictured before the name of the font.

2. You must click on the _____ _____ box on the Font dialog box to choose Fine, Small, Normal, Large, Very Large, or Extra Large type.

3. When you choose the Center command, a _____ _____ _____ _____ code is placed at the beginning of the line. A _____ _____ at the end of the line turns off centering.

4. To center just the page you are keying, click on Layout, Page, Center Page, and _____ _____.

5. _____ _____ should be used for aligning an entire section of text at the right.

6. To change to uppercase or lowercase after you have keyed some characters, you must use the Select feature and choose _____ and _____ _____.

Troubleshooting with Reveal Codes: Look at the codes below and determine what is wrong.

`[Bold]WordPerfect[Bold] for Windows.`

Why does all of the line not print in bold?

REVIEW EXERCISES

Each of these exercises gives you practice in applying many of the WordPerfect 6.0 for Windows attributes which you learned in the first five lessons. If you are not sure how to perform a certain function, look it up and study it carefully so that you will know how to do it in the future.

Key the document in Figure 5–4 exactly as it is shown. Do NOT format the document. Save this file with the name **success**.

▶ **REVIEW EXERCISE 5-1**

```
The common elements in success on the job are
exceptional performance in five competencies.  These
five competencies rest on a three-part foundation of
skills and personal qualities.  They are the hallmark
of today's expert worker.

The expert worker of tomorrow will not simply "pick
up" these competencies.  Their acquisition must begin
in the schools and be refined through on-the-job
experience and further training.  Teaching and
learning the competencies must become the tasks of our
schools and students. Competent workers demonstrate
their skill in managing or using:

1. Resources.  Workers schedule time, budget funds,
arrange space, or assign staff.

2. Interpersonal Skills.  Competent employees are
skilled team members and teachers of new workers; they
serve clients directly and persuade co-workers either
individually or in groups; they negotiate with others
to solve problems or reach decisions; they work
comfortably with colleagues from diverse backgrounds;
and they responsibly challenge existing procedures and
policies.

3. Information.  Workers are expected to identify,
assimilate, and integrate information from diverse
sources; they prepare, maintain, and interpret
quantitative and qualitative records; they convert
information from one form to another and are
comfortable conveying information, orally and in
writing, as the need arises.

4. Systems.  Workers should understand their own work
in the context of the work of those around them; they
understand how parts of systems are connected,
anticipate consequences, and monitor and correct their
own performance; they can identify trends and
anomalies in system performance, integrate multiple
```

> displays of data, and link symbols (e.g., displays on a computer screen) with real phenomena (e.g., machine performance).
>
> 5. Technology. Technology today is everywhere, demanding high levels of competence in selecting and using appropriate technology, visualizing operations, using technology to monitor tasks, and maintaining and troubleshooting complex equipment.

Figure 5-4

After you have saved the document, perform the following format changes:

1. Title this document `Competencies, Skills, and Personal Qualities`. Use a Times Roman (or something similar) 24 pt. font size and Center the title.
2. Double-space the first paragraph. Single-space the rest of the document.
3. Double-space between paragraphs.
4. Indent the numbered items so that all lines of text in these items begin at the same point.
5. Bold and Underline each of the five competencies (`Resources, Interpersonal Skills, Information, Systems, and Technology`).
6. Add your name, the current date, and your school name in Small type to be right aligned at the end of the document.
7. Center the document vertically on the page.
8. Save this document as **success.rev** to distinguish between the original and the revised document.
9. Print a copy and Close the file.

▶ **REVIEW EXERCISE 5-2**

Key the document shown in Figure 5-5 on the next page. Use Size and Appearance attributes, as well as the other features which enhance the appearance of a document, that you learned about in Lesson 5 to improve the appearance of this document.

1. Change the type size of `Thinking Skills` to E<u>x</u>tra Large and the remainder of the text to <u>V</u>ery Large.
2. Bold `Thinking Skills, Creative Thinking, Decision Making,` and the other major words at the beginning of each part.
3. Change the type size of the source at the bottom of the page to <u>S</u>mall.
4. Center the document on the page.
5. Save this document with the name **thinkskl.** Print a copy and Close the file.

LESSON 5   ENHANCING TEXT APPEARANCE   **WP79**

> THINKING SKILLS: Thinks creatively, makes decisions, solves problems, visualizes, knows how to learn, and reasons.
>
> A. Creative Thinking - generates new ideas.
>
> B. Decision Making - specifies goals and constraints, generates alternatives, considers risks, and evaluates and chooses best alternative.
>
> C. Problem Solving - recognizes problems and devises and implements plan of action.
>
> D. Seeing Things in the Mind's Eye - organizes and processes symbols, pictures, graphics, objects, and other information.
>
> E. Knowing How to Learn - uses efficient learning techniques to acquire and apply new knowledge and skills.
>
> F. Reasoning - discovers a rule or principle underlying the relationship between two or more objects and applies it in solving a problem.
>
> from WHAT WORK REQUIRES OF SCHOOLS, A SCANS REPORT FOR AMERICA 2000, p. xviii

▌ Figure 5-5

▶ **REVIEW EXERCISE 5-3**

1. Key the document shown in Figure 5-6. Since this is an invitation, it is appropriate to center each line and use italic.
2. If you have a variety of typefaces to choose from, pick one that looks appropriate for an invitation. Use as large a type size as you can appropriately use for the content and to fit on the page.
3. Center the document both vertically and horizontally on the page.
4. Save this document with the name **invit.** Print a copy and Close the file.

> A Celebration
>
> For: John and Jane Doe
>
> Date: November 21, 199-
>
> Time: Dinner served at 6 P.M.
>
> Place: Westwood Country Club in Middletown
>
> Given by: Their Children
>
> RSVP by: November 7, 199-
>
> It's A Surprise!
>
> No Gifts Please

▌ Figure 5-6

LESSON 6

Editing Features

OBJECTIVES

Upon completion of this lesson, you will be able to:

1. Cut, copy, and paste selected blocks.
2. Drag and drop text.
3. Find and replace text.
4. Use Hyphenation.

WordPerfect 6.0 for Windows provides many features which help to make editing easier and more enjoyable. In this lesson, you will learn about some especially useful features that will help you to make changes quickly.

CUT, COPY, AND PASTE

When you want to move text, you can make use of the Cut, Copy, and Paste commands found on the Power Bar and the Edit menu. To **Cut** means to remove the selected text from a document and place it in a holding place called the **Clipboard.** To **Copy** means to make a copy of selected text and to place it on the Clipboard (leaving the original text unchanged). You can then **Paste** the text from the Clipboard to a new location within that document, within another WordPerfect document, or within another Windows application.

Each time you cut or copy text, it replaces anything else that was on the Clipboard and stays there until you put something else on the Clipboard. This means that you can continue to paste the same text from the Clipboard again and again until you cut or copy something else. Any attributes (such as fonts and sizes) are placed on the Clipboard along with the selected text.

CUTTING AND PASTING TEXT

If you want to move a sentence in a paragraph, one method is to delete the sentence, and then rekey it. There is, however, a faster way:

- Select the block of text you want to cut (If you don't remember how to Select, review Lesson 2), and then
- Click on Cut on the Power Bar, or
- Choose the Edit menu and Cut, or press **Ctrl+X**.

The Selected text will disappear and be placed on the Clipboard, ready to be pasted. Move the Insertion Point to where you wish to place the sentence.

- Click on Paste on the Power Bar, or choose Edit and then Paste, or press **Ctrl+V**.

The sentence on the Clipboard will appear at the Insertion Point.

> **N O T E**
>
> If you have used Cut to delete text, you must use Paste to replace it. You can, however, use Undo to immediately reverse procedures such as Cut and Copy.

▶ **EXERCISE 6-1**

1. Open the file named **less1.wpd.**
2. Select the paragraph beginning with `Saving` and Cut and Paste it at the end of the document before `Your Name`.
3. Save the document as **less1.rev.** Close the file.

COPYING AND PASTING TEXT

When you copy text, you place a copy of the text on the Clipboard without removing the text from the document.

- Select the text that you want to copy.
- Click Copy on the Power Bar, or
- Choose Edit and then Copy, or press **Ctrl+C**.

The selected text is copied to the Clipboard, and the original text remains where it is. To place the selected text where you want it, move the Insertion Point to where you want the text copied.

- Click Paste on the Power Bar, or
- Choose Edit and then Paste, or press **Ctrl+V**.

Open the document named **less1.rev.** Copy and Paste `Your Name` so that it appears both at the beginning and near the end of the document. Save this document as **less2.rev.** Close the file.

▶ **EXERCISE 6-2**

DRAG AND DROP TEXT

WordPerfect 6.0 for Windows also provides the Drag and Drop Text feature to move or copy Selected text using only your mouse.

To use this feature, Select or highlight the text that you want to move, place the mouse pointer anywhere on the selected text, press and hold down the left mouse button, and drag to move the mouse pointer to the new location where you want to move or copy the text.

To move the text to the Insertion Point location, release the mouse button. To Copy the text to the Insertion Point location, hold the **Ctrl** key down any time before you release the mouse button.

If you move or Copy something by mistake, immediately choose Undo from the Edit menu.

FIND AND REPLACE

When editing, you may find yourself needing to change a specific word, phrase, or code. Instead of taking time to scroll through the document looking for that specific word, phrase, or code, you can use Find to move directly to the material you want.

The **Find** feature lets you search for any specified group of characters and/or codes in your document. The **Replace** feature lets you search for and replace any words, phrases, or codes.

FINDING A WORD, PHRASE, OR CODE

Begin by moving your Insertion Point to where you want the search to begin.

- Choose Edit and then Find.

The Find Text dialog box shown in Figure 6-1 will appear at the bottom of the screen. While this dialog box is open, you can use any of the main menus. If you Select text before opening the dialog box, the selection appears in the Find text box. Otherwise:

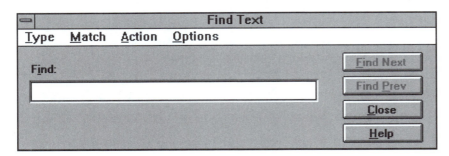

Figure 6-1
Find Text dialog box

1. To Find a word or phrase, key the text you want to find in the Find text box.

2. To Find any code, choose <u>M</u>atch and then C<u>o</u>des. The Codes dialog box shown in Figure 6-2 will appear. Select the code, choose Insert, and then choose Close to close the Codes dialog box.

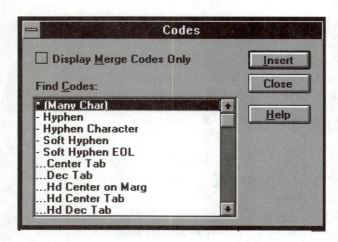

Figure 6-2
Codes dialog box

3. To find a specific code, choose <u>T</u>ype and then <u>S</u>pecific Codes. The Specific Codes dialog box shown in Figure 6–3 will appear. Select the code, choose OK, and then enter a specific value.

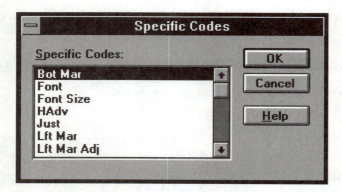

Figure 6-3
Specific Codes dialog box

WordPerfect 6.0 for Windows will automatically search forward from the Insertion Point unless you choose <u>O</u>ptions and make another choice.

Once you have keyed the text in the Find text box, you can choose <u>F</u>ind Next to find the next occurrence of the word, phrase, or code you want to find; or you can choose Find <u>P</u>rev to find the previous occurrence of the word, phrase, or code you want to find.

Choose <u>C</u>lose to return to your document.

📄 Open the document named **quote** and follow along carefully to use the Find feature.

▶ **EXERCISE 6-3**

1. With your Insertion Point at the beginning of the document, choose Edit and then Find. Key (SCANS) and press **Enter** or click on Find Next. (SCANS) will be highlighted in your document. Choose Close.

2. Choose Find. Key ", click on Find Next, and then click on Find Next again because there are both beginning and ending quotation marks in this document. Then choose Close.

3. Move the Insertion Point to the beginning of the document, and then choose Find, Match, and Codes. In the Find Codes list, highlight **HRt** and choose Insert and Close. Then choose Find Next and the location of the **HRt** code at the end of the first paragraph will be highlighted. Then choose Close.

4. This document has a double-indented paragraph for which we will find the code. Choose Find, Match, and Codes. Highlight **Hd Left/Right Ind** and choose Insert and Close. Then choose Find Next and the location of the **Hd Left/Right Ind** code will be highlighted. Then choose Close.

5. Finally, to choose a specific code, choose Find, Type, and Specific Codes. In the Specific Codes list, highlight **Rgt Mar** and choose OK. The Find Right Margin dialog box will appear, telling you that the right margin is 1". Choose Close.

6. Now Close this file. Do NOT save it.

REPLACING TEXT AND CODES

To replace text, move the Insertion Point to the place in the document where you want the replacing to begin.

- Choose Edit and then Replace.

Next, you complete the Find and Replace dialog box shown in Figure 6-4. Notice that this dialog box is similar to the Find dialog box, but it includes additional choices to be made.

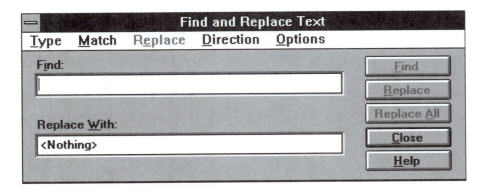

Figure 6-4
Find and Replace Text dialog box

Enter the text you wish to search for in the Find text box and press **Tab** to move from Find to Replace. Then enter the text you wish to replace the text with in the Replace With text box. Choose Direction and then choose the direction, Forward (down) or Backward (up), you wish to search from on the drop-down menu.

Click on Find if you want to find only the first occurrence of the find text; click on Replace if you want to replace the first occurrence of the search text. Then continue to look for the find text if selected again; or click on Replace All to replace every occurrence of the text from the Insertion Point to the beginning or end of the document, depending on the find direction.

If you want to delete the text or codes you are searching for, just leave the Replace With text box empty.

> **NOTE**
>
> When you use Replace All, you run the risk of replacing text you didn't mean to replace because all occurrences are not the same. The safest way to replace text is to use the Find and Replace options together so that you can check each replacement as it is made.

▶ EXERCISE 6-4

 Key the exercise shown in Figure 6-5, and save it with the name **document**. Then make the following changes:

1. Find all occurrences of `WordPerfect for Windows` and replace them with `WordPerfect 6.0 for Windows`.

2. Find all the Left Tab codes and Replace them with nothing.

3. Save the document as **document.rev** and close the file.

```
   Each user of WordPerfect for Windows should be
familiar with the documentation (printed materials)
shipped with the WordPerfect for Windows software.  If
you are in a company which provides computer support,
you may need to look at the documentation only
occasionally.  However, if you are in a small company
(or operating your own home computer) where you have
to do everything with the computer yourself, you will
find the documentation to be invaluable.

   This documentation will tell you how to install the
new WordPerfect for Windows on your computer and how
to load the printer drivers you will need.  The
documentation includes an overview of how the
WordPerfect for Windows software operates through a
series of self-paced lessons.  In addition, you will
find the WordPerfect for Windows Reference or User's
Guide helpful whenever you run into a problem.  It is
easy to find what you need to know because it is
organized alphabetically.
```

▎Figure 6-5

HYPHENATION

You may have noticed that automatic word wrap can cause some unattractive gaps and spaces at the end of lines in your left–justified text by forcing a long word down to the next line, or in fully justified text by leaving very wide spaces between words. To make the text at the right margin more even or to eliminate some of the extra spaces between words, you can turn on Hyphenation. WordPerfect 6.0 for Windows will automatically hyphenate those words which are in the WordPerfect dictionary. To turn on Hyphenation, position the Insertion Point where you want hyphenation to begin.

- Choose Layout, Line, and Hyphenation.

The Line Hyphenation dialog box will appear, as shown in Figure 6-6. The Hyphenation Zone determines when WordPerfect will hyphenate a word. If Hyphenation On is checked, a word that extends into or beyond this Hyphenation Zone will be hyphenated. The options in the Hyphenation Zone can be modified, but the default settings will generally suffice.

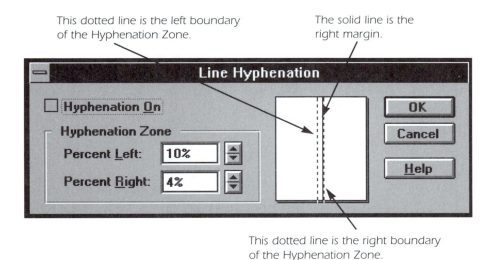

Figure 6-6
Line Hyphenation dialog box

- Choose Hyphenation On, and then OK.

The code **[Hyph]** is placed in your text at the Insertion Point location. The text following the code will be hyphenated at the end of a line, if appropriate.

Open the file named **recycle1.wpd.** Make the following editing changes in the document:

1. Change the font to Arial 12 pt. or something similar.
2. Turn on Hyphenation.
3. Select the side heading `Paper` and the paragraph which follows it. Cut this section and Paste it to appear at the end of the document.
4. Copy the phrase at the beginning of the document, `Recycle Beginning Today!`, and Paste it to appear at the end of the document as well as at the beginning of the document.
5. Center the phrase `Recycle Beginning Today!` at the beginning of the document.
6. Find the word `recycle` and Replace it with `Recycle Beginning Today` where appropriate.
7. Save the file as **recycle3,** Print a copy, and Close the file.

REVIEW

TRUE/FALSE

Circle the correct answer.

1. T F To Copy means to make a copy of Selected or highlighted text and to place it on the Clipboard (leaving the original text unchanged).

2. T F Each time you Cut or Copy text, it replaces anything else that was on the Clipboard and stays there until you put something else on the Clipboard.

3. T F Any attributes, such as fonts and sizes, are lost when placed on the Clipboard.

4. T F You can use Undo to reverse procedures such as Cut or Copy.

5. T F You can find and replace through the same dialog box.

6. T F If Hyphenation On is checked, a word that would be wrapped and that falls within the Hyphenation Zone will not be hyphenated.

COMPLETION

Fill in the blank.

1. To _____ means to remove Selected text from a document and place it in a holding place called the Clipboard.

2. You can _____ the text from the Clipboard to a new location within that document, within another WordPerfect document, or within another Windows application.

3. You will always begin either Cutting or Copying a block of text by _____ it.

4. If you have used Cut to delete text, use _____ to place it.

5. The _____ feature lets you search for any specified group of characters and/or codes in your document.

6. To make the text more even at the right margin or to eliminate some of the extra spaces between words, you would use _____.

Troubleshooting with Reveal Codes: Describe what would happen to your document if you discover a **[Hyph]** code halfway through the document.

LESSON 7

ExpressDocs Templates

OBJECTIVES

Upon completion of this chapter, you will be able to:

1. Use a template to prepare a letter.
2. Use a template to prepare a memo.
3. Use a template to prepare a class schedule.
4. Use a template to prepare a certificate.

A **template** is a predesigned layout for a document which can be used repeatedly to create other documents of the same type. You can use the templates that WordPerfect has created or you can create your own templates. The templates provided with WordPerfect are called **ExpressDocs** and have the file extension of .wpt.

The default template, called **standard,** is in effect each time you start WordPerfect. This template automatically provides you with a blank screen, one-inch top, bottom, right, and left margins, tabs set at every one-half inch, and other default settings.

You can also open other template documents to which different Button Bars may be attached as well as even a different set of pull–down menus. Templates may be as simple as a memo or as complicated as a newsletter containing various formatting styles.

USING TEMPLATES

WordPerfect 6.0 for Windows includes a variety of predefined templates. Whenever you open a template, you will be prompted for information.

Throughout this lesson, you are to perform a series of exercises in which you will learn to work with templates. Follow along carefully.

1. Beginning with a blank screen, choose File and then Template, OR press the Template button on the Button Bar. The Templates dialog box shown in Figure 7-1 will appear. A list of templates is included in the Document Template to Use box, and at the bottom of the dialog box you will find a brief description of each of the templates. When the dialog box first appears, "standard" will be highlighted and a brief description of this standard template appears.

▶ EXERCISE 7-1

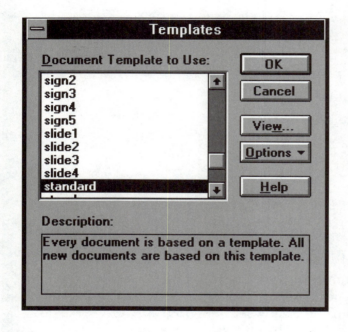

Figure 7-1
Template dialog box

2. Highlight each of the following templates and note the description provided. (You will have to use the up and down arrows OR the Scroll Bars to find all of these.)

   standard, cal_side, classchd, memo3, and resume

3. Now highlight **letter1,** and this time click OK to open the Template Information dialog box.

4. Click on the Personal Information button at the right of the Template Information dialog box, and in the Enter Your Personal Information box, key the information shown in Figure 7-2 on the next page. (Key your information right over any other information that may be there.) Press

N O T E

If this is the first time the templates software has been used, the Personal Information dialog box will come up automatically.

WP92 LESSON 7 EXPRESSDOCS TEMPLATES

Tab as you complete a box or click on Ne**x**t Field so that WordPerfect will move you automatically to the next box. Click on OK when you have completed the boxes.

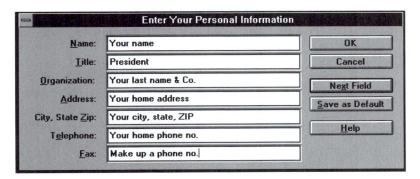

Figure 7-2
Personal Information dialog box

5. The Template Information dialog box will appear. Key your responses in all of the boxes as shown in Figure 7-3.

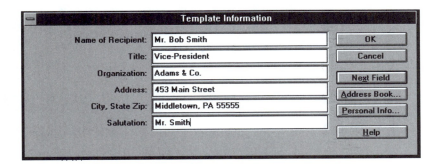

Figure 7-3
Template Information dialog box

As you complete each box, be sure to press **Tab** OR click on Ne**x**t Field so that WordPerfect will move you to the next box. If necessary, use the mouse pointer to take you back to fill a box before you click on OK. When you have keyed all entries correctly, click on OK.

6. The template, including your entries, now appears along with a different set of icons on the Button Bar. All you have to do is key the body of the letter. Key the paragraphs shown in Figure 7-4 on the next page.

> I have been using the templates and have found what great timesavers they can be! Once you get used to working with them, you will want to use them all the time. Even though it takes a few minutes to fill in the dialog boxes, you will find that, since you don't have to key that information in again on your document, using a template will help you produce a document faster.
>
> You have already learned to use the icons on the Button Bar for some of your applications. You will use even more of the Button Bar icons when you use the templates because a new Button Bar, especially suited to the template you have opened, will appear.
>
> Try using the ExpressDocs templates. You will be glad you did!

Figure 7-4

7. Save this document as **template.let** and Print a copy. Close the document. Note that the screen has gone back to the original Button Bar.

Next, you will open another template. Note that each template has its own Button Bar and has a different Template dialog box.

▶ **EXERCISE 7-2**

1. Open the **memo3** template. Click on Personal Information and, if necessary, enter the information shown in Figure 7-2. Then choose OK. Key all of your responses in the Template Information dialog box as follows and click on OK.

    | Name of Recipient: | Your teacher's name |
    | cc: *(courtesy carbon copy)* | (Since you do not need a cc, leave this blank.) |
    | Subject: | More information on templates |

2. When the template appears, key the paragraphs shown in Figure 7-5.

> The more I use templates, the more I see how useful they can be. Some other information that is important to know about templates follows:
>
> If you frequently send letters, memos, and faxes to the same people, you can store the information for these people in the Address Book option by clicking on that button. You can save even more time by using the Address Book for frequently used names and addresses.
>
> Templates are formatted with the Bitstream TrueType fonts that are included with WordPerfect 6.0 for Windows. If these have not been installed, WordPerfect will try to find the closest match to the fonts you have available.

Figure 7-5

3. Save this document as **template.mem** and Print a copy. Close the document.

The following exercises provide you with an opportunity to try two more of the templates provided in WordPerfect 6.0 for Windows.

▶ **EXERCISE 7-3**

Open the template named **classchd** and fill in your class schedule for the present term. To add extra rows to the table, place the Insertion Point in the last cell (the box at the far right of the bottom row) and then press **Tab.** Save this document as **classchd.me.** Print and Close this document.

▶ **EXERCISE 7-4**

Open the template named **certif2.** In the box for Name of Recipient, enter the name of your best friend. In the Description of Award box, key `The best friend a person could have!` Press **Enter** or choose OK. Since this certificate is in landscape format, that is sideways on the paper, use the Page Full Zoom button on the Power Bar to look at it. Then Save this document as **certif.frd.** Print and Close this document.

As you can see, the ExpressDocs templates can be very useful and help you to be much more productive. You will find many ways to use them in the future. If you need to create your own templates, you will find that WordPerfect 6.0 for Windows provides you with directions in the Reference documentation and in the ExpressDocs booklet.

REVIEW

TRUE/FALSE

Circle the correct answer.

1. T F The templates provided with WordPerfect have the file extension of .wpt.

2. T F Every document you create is based on a template.

3. T F Different templates may have different Button Bars, macros, and pull-down menus.

4. T F A list of templates is included in the Document Template to Use box.

5. T F WordPerfect comes with a number of templates.

6. T F The icons on the Button Bar may change as you use different templates.

COMPLETION

Fill in the blank.

1. A _____ is a predesigned layout for a document which can be used repeatedly to create other documents of the same type.

2. The _____ template is automatically provided to you when you start WordPerfect.

3. Most templates will have their own _____ _____ to prompt you for information for that template.

4. You can edit the personal information you have entered by choosing _____ _____ from the Template Information box.

5. A _____ of each template appears at the bottom of the Template dialog box.

6. Another name sometimes used to describe the templates provided within the WordPerfect software is _____.

Reference Question: Look at the ExpressDocs booklet which comes as a part of the WordPerfect 6.0 for Windows documentation. Note all the many different kinds of templates available to you. List the six categories of templates available.

LESSON 8

Multi-page Documents and Printing

OBJECTIVES

Upon completion of this lesson, you will be able to:

1. Insert files to assemble a document.
2. Print page numbers on a document.
3. Use expandable codes in Reveal Codes.
4. Keep text together: Widow/Orphan, Block Protect, Conditional End of Page.
5. Print headers and footers on a document.
6. Suppress page numbers, headers, and footers.
7. Use Go To.
8. Print selected pages, multiple pages, and copies.

WordPerfect 6.0 for Windows contains many features for managing multi-page documents, such as reports, term papers, or letters. In this lesson, you will learn about many of these features which will help make your job easier when you prepare long documents.

MULTI-PAGE DOCUMENTS

Sometimes you will key a long document all at one time. At other times you may retrieve or assemble various parts of a document from previously stored material. This is known as **document assembly**.

INSERTING A DOCUMENT FILE INTO AN EXISTING WINDOW

When you insert a document file, the inserted document file is placed into the active (currently open) window at the Insertion Point. This is a useful feature to use where you want to combine documents. For example, several different people may have gathered information and written parts of a report. When you prepare the final report, you can bring each independently developed section into the final report by using the Insert File feature.

To insert a document, make sure the document you wish to insert the material *into* is in the active window. Position the Insertion Point where you want to insert the text which is to be retrieved. *(Pay attention to spacing and layout.)*

- Choose Insert and then File.

The Insert File dialog box will appear. Enter the file name of the document or use the file lists to select the file. Once the file name is identified:

- Choose Insert.

If part of a document is already on your screen, a message will ask if you are sure you want to "Insert file into current document?"

- Select Yes to continue or No to stop the process.

▶ **EXERCISE 8-1**

To complete this exercise, you will use the files you saved earlier, named **quote.wpd, basic.wpd,** and **success.wpd.** You will assemble a report from these three documents. You need to perform the following steps:

1. As is customary on the first page of a report, you should leave a top margin of 2" and key the centered title, `Preparation for the Future`.

2. Double-space, and then Insert the document file named **quote.wpd.**

3. Move the Insertion Point a single space below that document, key the side heading `Basic Skills`, and press **Enter.** Insert the document file named **basic.wpd.** At the end of the document, Delete the text shown in parentheses.

4. Move the Insertion Point a single space below that document, key the side heading `Success`, and press **Enter.** Insert the document file named **success.wpd.**

Some reformatting is needed in the assembled document. Perform the following steps:

5. Convert the title to uppercase and bold the title and the two side headings.

6. Underline each of the five competencies (`Resources`, `Interpersonal Skills`, `Information`, `Systems`, and `Technology`).

7. Run the Speller.

8. Review and edit the total document so that the entire document is double-spaced, except after the title, which will be followed by three blank lines, and the quotation, which should be single-spaced.

9. Indent the first line of each new paragraph .5" (including the quotation).

10. In the `Success` section of the document, Indent each of the numbered items from both the left and right. And then Indent the numbered items so that all lines of text in the items begin at the same point.

11. Note that in the Title Bar, this document is still not titled, so you should Save the new document with the name **docassem.**

12. Print a copy of the report and Close the file.

USING PAGE NUMBERS

When you have a long document with multiple pages, you will usually want to include page numbers. Position the Insertion Point somewhere on the page where you want the page numbering to begin.

1. Open the **docassem.wpd** file. To number the entire document, move to the beginning of the document.

2. Choose Layout, Page, and then Numbering. The Page Numbering dialog box shown in Figure 8-1 will appear.

EXERCISE 8-2

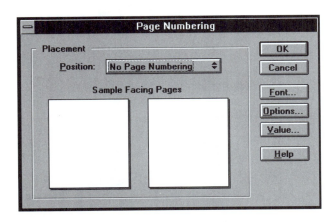

Figure 8-1
Page Numbering dialog box

3. Choose Position to display the choices shown in Figure 8-2, and click on Bottom Center. When you choose a page number Position, the Sample Facing Pages show how the numbers would appear on the page.

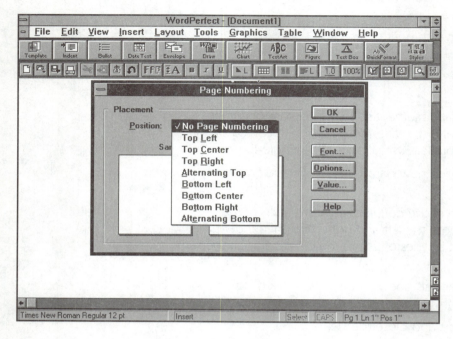

Figure 8-2
Page Number Position Choices

4. After you make your choice, choose OK to close the dialog box and return to the document. Do not Close this document.

SUPPRESSING A PAGE NUMBER

Sometimes you want page numbering for a document but you do not want a number to appear on a particular page, such as the first page. In such situations, you ask WordPerfect to suppress the page number for a particular page.

Follow the steps below to suppress page numbering for the first page of the **docassem.wpd** document:

EXERCISE 8-3

1. Move the Insertion Point to the first page if you are not already there.
2. Choose Layout, Page, and then Suppress. The Suppress dialog box shown in Figure 8-3 will appear.

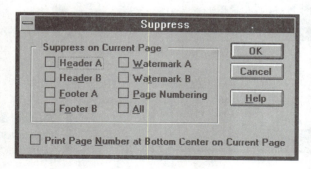

Figure 8-3
Suppress dialog box

WP102 LESSON 8 MULTI-PAGE DOCUMENTS AND PRINTING

3. Check the **P**age Numbering box in order to suppress page numbering for the current page.
4. Choose OK to return to the document.
5. Do not Close this file.

SETTING NEW NUMBERS

If you have created documents that have chapters or lessons (such as this textbook), you can create and save each lesson separately but number the complete document sequentially. To do this, move the Insertion Point to the page where you want to set a new page number.

- Choose **L**ayout, **P**age, and **N**umbering, and then click on **V**alue.

The Numbering Value dialog box will appear, and you can specify a New Page Number. Choose OK to return to the Page Numbering dialog box, and then choose Close to return to the document window.

EXPANDABLE CODES IN REVEAL CODES

Some codes are **expandable codes.** In Reveal Codes, when you click on the code or when the Insertion Point is positioned immediately in front of the code, the code will expand and provide more detailed information.

When you use the Suppress Page Numbering feature, the code **[Suppress]** will be inserted. When you click on this expanded code, it will expand and display **[Suppress:Page Num]**. The **[Pg Num Fmt]** and **[Pg Num Pos]** codes are also both expandable codes.

KEEPING TEXT TOGETHER

Use **Widow/Orphan, Block Protect,** and **Conditional End of Page** to keep text together on one page.

WIDOWS AND ORPHANS

A **widow** occurs when there is room at the bottom of a page for only the first line of a paragraph and the rest of the paragraph is forced to the next page. An **orphan** occurs when there is no room for the last line of a paragraph and it is forced to the next page. A single line of a paragraph at the bottom or the top of a page is not desirable and should be avoided if possible.

Turning on the Widow/Orphan feature guards against widows by forcing the first line of a paragraph to the next page so that it is kept with the rest of the paragraph, and it guards against orphans by taking the last two lines of a paragraph to the next page.

To turn on Widow/Orphan protection, move the Insertion Point to the place where you want to start preventing widows and orphans (usually the top of a document).

- Choose Layout, Page, and Keep Text Together; then select Prevent the first and last lines of paragraphs from being separated across pages, and choose OK.

BLOCK PROTECT

You should use **Block Protect** to keep a section of text from being divided between two pages. When you work with a table or document where the number of lines is constantly increasing or decreasing, text you want to keep all together on one page may be split so it spans two pages. Block Protect lets you keep the text together as long as the text you are protecting is less than a page in length.

To use Block Protect, Select the text you want to protect. Then:

- Choose Layout, Page, and Keep Text Together; then select Keep selected text together on same page, and choose OK.

CONDITIONAL END OF PAGE

You should use **Conditional End of Page** to keep a specific number of lines together on one page. For example, you can use Conditional End of Page to keep a title and its following paragraph together on the same page.

To use Conditional End of Page, move the Insertion Point to the beginning of the text you want to keep together. Then:

- Choose Layout, Page, and Keep Text Together. Select Number of lines to keep together, and then specify the number of lines you want to keep together. (When you specify the number of lines to keep together, remember to include any blank lines.) Then choose OK.

Continuing to work with the file **docassem.wpd,** prevent widows/orphans. Save this document as **docassem.rev.** Print a copy and Close the file. Notice how the page numbers printed.

► EXERCISE 8-4

HEADERS AND FOOTERS

Headers and footers can add a professional touch to the appearance of a document. Text that is repeated at the top of every page is called a header. Text repeated at the bottom is a footer. Headers are printed at the top of the page just below the top margin. Footers are printed at the bottom of the page, just above the bottom margin.

A common application of a header is to include the title of the report, the page number, and the current date. If you are working on the draft of a document, you could use a footer to print the word "Draft" at the bottom of each page so that nobody will confuse the draft with the final document.

CREATING A HEADER OR FOOTER

Notice that both headers and footers are created in the same way. You should be in Page or Two-Page view since headers and footers do not display in Draft view.

Position the Insertion Point in the first paragraph on the page where you want the header or footer to begin. Then:

- Choose Layout and then Header/Footer.

The Headers/Footers dialog box shown in Figure 8-4 will appear. Note that the dialog box contains Header A and B as well as Footer A and B, which makes it possible for you to have two headers and two footers in a document. A and B will appear on separate lines.

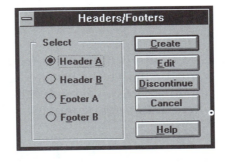

Figure 8-4
Headers/Footers dialog box

- Click on Header A or Footer A; then choose Create.

The additional bar which appears, shown in Figure 8-5, is known as a **Feature Bar.** A Feature Bar is used to show you additional options available for a feature. The header will appear at the flashing Insertion Point.

Figure 8-5
Headers/Footers Feature Bar

- Key the text of the header or footer.

You can use any of the attributes (such as center, bold, flush right, italic, etc.), and you can edit the text as you normally would using any of the WordPerfect editing features.

LESSON 8   MULTI-PAGE DOCUMENTS AND PRINTING   **WP105**

- Click on Placement on the Feature Bar and select the pages (even, odd, or every) where you want the header or footer to appear.
- Click on Distance on the Feature Bar.

The Distance dialog box will appear. Here you can key the distance which you wish WordPerfect to leave between the header or footer and the body text. The default distance (0.167") is about one blank line between the header or footer and the body text, so you would click on OK.

- Choose Close to close the header or footer and return to the document.

You can change the font and font size of the header or footer by clicking on the icons on the Power Bar. If you do not change the font in a header or footer, it prints in the font that is current where the header or footer is created.

The Header code and the Footer code are both expandable in Reveal Codes.

INCLUDING THE DATE IN A HEADER OR FOOTER

You can use almost every WordPerfect feature in a header or footer, including the Date feature. While creating the header or footer, move the Insertion Point to the place where the date is to be inserted.

- Choose Insert and then Date.

Choose Date Text if you want to insert the date as regular text, or choose Date Code if you want the date to be updated each time you open or print the documents. Finish keying the header or footer and choose Close to return to the document.

INCLUDING A PAGE NUMBER IN A HEADER OR FOOTER

Headers and footers can include page numbers. In fact, if you want to print both a page number and a header or footer, it is easier to include the page number with the header or footer text in a manner such as the following:

```
199- Annual Report          -3-          XYZ Corporation
Lesson 7                                          Page 5
```

To do this, key the text of the header or footer, and when you reach the point where the page number is to appear, choose Number from the Feature Bar, and then click on Page Number. The code [PgNum Disp] will be inserted, indicating where the page number will be displayed when the document is printed.

If you set up a header or footer and turn on page numbering in the same part of the page, they may overlap when your document is printed. Therefore, it is better to include the page numbers inside a header or footer.

1. Open the file named **docassem.wpd**.

2. Change to Left justification (if necessary).
3. Apply Widow/Orphan protection, Block Protect, and Conditional End of Page to keep text together as appropriate.
4. Create the following header across the top of the page:

`Preparing for Success     page no.     Current Date`

5. Create the following footer:

`Draft` (printed at the left margin)

6. Click on the Close button on the Feature Bar.
7. Suppress printing the header on page 1.
8. Save the document as **docassem.hf**.
9. Close the document.

EDITING A HEADER OR FOOTER

You can make changes to an existing header or footer by following these steps. With Page or Two-Page view selected:

- Choose Layout and then Header/Footer.
- Choose the header or footer you would like to edit (A or B).
- Choose Edit.

The header or footer will appear on the screen. Edit the header or footer as you normally would perform editing.

- Choose Close when you are finished to return to your document. You can also click anywhere in the document window (outside the header or footer) to return to your document.

SUPPRESSING A HEADER OR FOOTER

You can suppress a header or footer on a particular page as follows:

- Choose Layout, Page, and Suppress.
- Choose the headers or footers you want to suppress. You can choose All to select all the items.
- Choose OK.

Open the file named **docassem.hf**.

1. Edit the header by Selecting the title `Preparing for Success` and converting it to uppercase.
2. Edit the footer by Selecting the word `Draft` and converting it to uppercase.

3. Save the document as **docassem.hfe.**

4. Close the document.

THE GO TO COMMAND

A feature which may be very useful when editing is the Go To command. The Go To command can be used to move the Insertion Point quickly to a specific location in your document if you take the following steps:

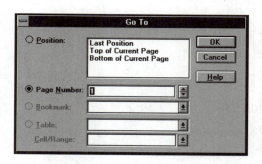

Figure 8-6
Go To dialog box

- Click on Edit and Go To, or press **Ctrl+G.**

The dialog box shown in Figure 8-6 will appear, displaying the current page number.

- Key the page number which you wish to go to or select from the other choices provided.

- Click on OK.

1. Open the document named **docassem.wpd.**
2. Choose Edit and Go To.
3. Key 3 in the Page Number box and press **Enter.**
4. Close the file.

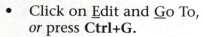

EXERCISE 8-7

As you can see, the Go To feature can be especially useful when you are working with large documents.

PRINTING

After creating a document, you will usually want to print it right away, as you learned to do in Lesson 1. However, WordPerfect offers many printing options which help you perform printing easily and quickly.

When you are working with multi-page documents, you may need to print a single page or a range of pages, rather than the full document. WordPerfect provides several options for this through the Print dialog box.

PRINTING THE CURRENT PAGE

Move the Insertion Point to the page to be printed. *(Make sure the Insertion Point itself is located on that page, not just the mouse pointer.)*

- Click on the Print button to obtain the Print dialog box. (See Figure 8-7.)

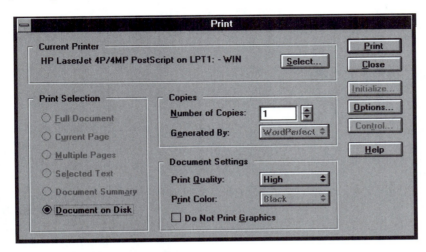

Figure 8-7
Print dialog box

- Choose the Current Page (the page that contains the Insertion Point) option.

- Print the page by selecting Print.

PRINTING A SELECTED PAGE OR RANGE OF PAGES

If you want to print selected pages from a document, you can use the Multiple Pages option in the Print dialog box. When the Print dialog box appears:

- Choose the Multiple Pages option, and then choose Print.

The Multiple Pages dialog box shown in Figure 8-8 will appear, requesting the pages to be printed. Enter the page numbers for the pages to be printed, following the pattern shown here:

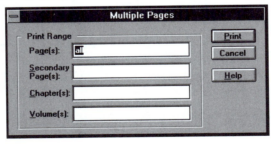

Figure 8-8
Multiple Pages dialog box

If you enter:	This will print:
5	Page 5
2,6,12	Selected pages (2, 6, and 12)
1–5	A range of pages (1 through 5)

LESSON 8   MULTI-PAGE DOCUMENTS AND PRINTING   **WP109**

1–5,12	A range of pages (1 through 5) and a selected page (12)
6–	From page 6 to the end of the document

- Choose OK to print the pages, *or* press Cancel if you do not wish to print.

Notice that entering numbers for nonexistent pages does not cause any problems; pages that do not exist are simply not printed.

PRINTING MORE THAN ONE COPY

Through the Print dialog box, you can specify the number of copies to be printed.

- Choose <u>N</u>umber of Copies and enter the number of copies to be printed. Then select <u>P</u>rint.

▶ **EXERCISE 8-8**

Print two copies of page 2 of the document you have named **docassem.hfe**. Close the file.

▶ **EXERCISE 8-9**

Open the file you saved in REVIEW EXERCISE 3-1 as **recycle.wpd**. Upon review, you can see several items that should be changed:

1. At the beginning of the document, leave a top margin of approximately 2" above the title by spacing down 1". (Hint: Watch the status line while pressing **Enter.**)

2. Bold and center the title and double-space after it.

3. Bold and put in uppercase each of the side headings, `Paper`, `Glass`, `Cans & Metal`, and `Plastics`.

4. Indent the beginning of each paragraph .5 ".

5. Center the group of lines beginning `Clear`, `Amber`, and `Green` and the group of lines beginning `Beverage Cans`, `Steel Cans`, and `Household Aluminum`.

6. Double-space the document.

7. Go to the beginning of the document and turn on Widow/Orphan protection.

8. Create the following header across the top of the page:

RECYCLE BEGINNING TODAY!   page no.   Current Date

9. Suppress the printing of the header on the first page.

10. Save the document as **recycle4.**

11. Print one copy and Close the file.

REVIEW

TRUE/FALSE

Circle the correct answer.

1. T F When you insert a document file, the document file is placed into the active (currently open) window at the Insertion Point.

2. T F When you choose Page and Numbering from the Layout menu, the Page Numbering code is automatically placed at the beginning of the document.

3. T F You can instruct WordPerfect to suppress the printing of a page number, header, or footer on a particular page.

4. T F You can use Conditional End of Page to keep a title and its following paragraph together on the same page.

5. T F One-half inch is automatically inserted between headers or footers and the body text.

6. T F WordPerfect permits you to print a single page or a range of pages.

COMPLETION

Fill in the blank.

1. _____ _____ is the process of assembling various parts of a document from previously stored material.

2. You can set the page number you want to start numbering with by moving the Insertion Point to the page where you want to set a new page and choosing Layout, Page, Numbering, and _____.

3. You should use _____ _____ to keep a section of text from being divided between two pages.

4. A(n) _____ occurs when there is room at the bottom of a page for only the first line of a paragraph and the rest of the paragraph is forced to the next page.

5. A(n) _____ occurs when there is no room for the last line of a paragraph and it is forced to the next page.

6. To move the Insertion Point very quickly to a specific page, use the _____ _____ command.

Troubleshooting with Reveal Codes: The page numbers are printing at the bottom left side of the page instead of in the bottom center. When you look in Reveal Codes, you see **[Pg Num Pos]**, which doesn't tell you what the problem is. What should you do?

LESSON 9

Footnotes, Endnotes, Thesaurus, and Grammatik

OBJECTIVES

Upon completion of this lesson, you will be able to:
1. Use footnotes and endnotes.
2. Use the Thesaurus.
3. Use Grammatik.
4. Use Document Information.

FOOTNOTES AND ENDNOTES

Multi-page documents, which you learned to handle in Lesson 8, often include footnotes or endnotes. Footnotes and endnotes are useful for providing the source of material used in the document or for providing a more detailed explanation of material found in the document.

When you create footnotes using the Footnote feature, WordPerfect automatically numbers them, places them at the bottom of the appropriate page, and adjusts the page length accordingly. Endnotes may be found at the end of a paper or a chapter. You can edit, add, or delete footnotes or endnotes anywhere in the body of the document. WordPerfect will automatically renumber and reformat all such notes if you add or delete notes.

CREATING A FOOTNOTE OR ENDNOTE

To create a footnote, move the Insertion Point to the place in the document where you want to insert the reference number for the new footnote or endnote. Then:

- Choose Insert, Footnote, and Create.

If you want to create an endnote, you would choose Endnote instead of Footnote. As you key the text of the footnote (or endnote), you can edit the text as you normally would, using any of the available WordPerfect editing features.

A Feature Bar with four buttons will appear. (The Endnote Feature Bar is identical. Feature Bars provide easy access to options related to a specific feature.) On this Feature Bar, click on Note Number to restore the note number if you delete it; click on Next or Previous to move to the next or previous note.

- Click on Close to close the note.

Choose Close when finished, and you will automatically be returned to the body of the document.

The superscript footnote or endnote number will automatically appear in the text of your document. The Insertion Point will automatically move to the footnote position at the foot of the page or to the endnote position at the end of the document. A two-inch horizontal line will be inserted automatically to separate the footnotes from the regular text. If you are using Page view, you can see the line and footnote by clicking on the Page Zoom Full button.

Both the Endnote and Footnote codes are expandable in Reveal Codes.

Key the short document shown in Figure 9-1 on the next page, using the Footnote feature when you see the superscripted numbers. Save the document with the name **phone.** Print a copy and Close the file.

> On March 7, 1876, the first telephone patent (No. 174,465) was issued to a professor of vocal physiology at Boston University who had been previously spurned by Mark Twain as an inventor.[1] Professor Bell would no doubt have been incredulous at the prediction that 100 years later, there would be 153 million telephones in the United States,[2] along with terms like PBX (private branch exchange), Centrex, BOC (Bell operating companies), ACD (automatic call distribution), voice mailboxes, and cellular phones.
>
> ───────────────
>
> [1]Bell, Alexander Graham, "Research in Telephony," Proceedings of the American Academy of Arts and Sciences, 1876; 12:1-10.
>
> [2]"The Telephone." Collier's Encyclopedia, Macmillan Educational Corp., New York, 1969; 22:121-133.

Figure 9-1

Footnotes will be printed at the foot of the page, regardless of the amount of text on the page, unless you indicate through the Options that they are to be placed below the text. To do this, choose Insert, Footnote, and Options and the Footnote Options dialog box shown in Figure 9-2 will appear. Choose Place Notes Below Text. WordPerfect then will automatically position your footnotes below the text.

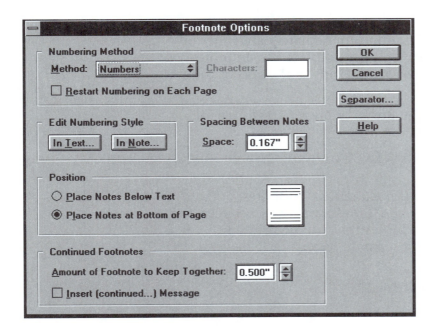

Figure 9-2
Footnote Options dialog box.

EDITING A FOOTNOTE OR ENDNOTE

To make changes to a footnote or endnote:

- Choose Insert, Footnote (or Endnote), and then Edit. Key the number of the footnote (or endnote) to be edited and choose OK.

If you are using Page view, you can also click on the text of the footnote or endnote to edit it right on the Page view screen.

The note will be displayed on the screen so that you can see it as you make any necessary changes. Edit the text as you normally would, using any of the available editing features. Note that you can also choose Next or Previous to edit the next or previous footnote (or endnote). If you accidentally delete the note number while editing the note, choose Note Number to reinsert it. (The number is deleted only from the footnote itself—not from the text in the document.)

- Choose Close to confirm your changes and return to the document.

▶ **EXERCISE 9-2**

After you key the exercise named **phone,** you realize that you mistakenly indicated that the Collier's Encyclopedia was published in 1969. Edit the footnote so that it will read correctly as 1979. Change this document so that the footnotes are placed below the text rather than at the bottom of the page. Save the document as **phone2** and Close the file.

CHOOSING WHERE TO PLACE ENDNOTES

WordPerfect normally prints endnotes immediately after the text at the end of the document. If you want to place the endnotes on a separate page, move the Insertion Point to the end of the document.

- Choose Insert and then Page Break, *or* press **Ctrl+Enter** for a page break.
- Choose Layout, Line, and then Center to center the heading for the endnote page.
- Key a heading for the page (for example, "Endnotes,"). Press **Enter** two or three times to add a few blank lines between the title of the page and the endnotes that will be printed there. Now your endnotes are on a separate page.

USING A HARD PAGE BREAK

Most multi-page documents require a title page. Many people prepare the title page as the last page of a long document.

When it is keyed as the last page of a document, you will want it to start on a new page. To start a new page (using a hard page break):

- Choose the Insert menu, and then choose Page Break or press **Ctrl+Enter.**

A hard page break is shown as **[HPg]** when Reveal Codes is on. You can delete a hard page break by positioning the Insertion Point immediately after it and pressing Backspace.

If you put the title page at the end of a multi-page document, you will need to suppress the printing of any page numbering and headers or footers onto it. Also, for an attractive title page, the contents should be centered both vertically and horizontally.

You can design your own title page or you can use one of the several provided in the templates.

Open the file named **docassem.rev.** Insert footnotes as follows, using the Footnote feature:

1. At the end of the quotation at the end of the second paragraph:

   ¹LEARNING A LIVING: A BLUEPRINT FOR HIGH PERFORMANCE, A SCANS Report for America 2000, The Secretary's Commission on Achieving Necessary Skills, U.S. Department of Labor, April 1992, p. v.

2. At the end of the first paragraph of the section subtitled Success:

   ²WHAT WORK REQUIRES OF SCHOOLS, A SCANS Report for America 2000, The Secretary's Commission on Achieving Necessary Skills, U.S. Department of Labor, June 1991, p. 11.

3. After the last word at the end of the text:

   ³Ibid., pp. 11-13.

4. As the last page of the document, create your own title page with the title PREPARATION FOR THE FUTURE. Add to the title page: your name, your instructor's name, and the date. Suppress page numbering on the first page and the title page.

5. Save this document as **docassem.ftn.** Print the entire document and Close the file.

Open the file named **docassem.rev.** Insert endnotes as follows, using the Endnote feature:

1. At the end of the quotation at the end of the second paragraph:

   1. LEARNING A LIVING: A BLUEPRINT FOR HIGH PERFORMANCE, A SCANS Report for America 2000, The Secretary's Commission on Achieving Necessary Skills, U.S. Department of Labor, April 1992, p. v.

2. At the end of the first paragraph of the section subtitled Success:

   ```
   2. WHAT WORK REQUIRES OF SCHOOLS, A SCANS Report
   for America 2000. The Secretary's Commission on
   Achieving Necessary Skills, U.S. Department of
   Labor, June 1991, p. 11.
   ```

3. After the last word at the end of the text:

   ```
   3. Ibid., pp. 11-13.
   ```

4. Prepare a separate page for the endnotes with the title ENDNOTES.
5. Suppress page numbering on the first page.
6. Save this document as **docassem.end** and Close the file.

▶ **EXERCISE 9-5**

1. Choose one of the ExpressDocs title page templates and prepare a title page for the document with the title PREPARATION FOR THE FUTURE. Prepare the title page for your instructor.
2. Print and Save the file as **title.pge.** Close the file.

USING THE THESAURUS

The Thesaurus feature of WordPerfect is designed to help you write a document. The WordPerfect Thesaurus searches for and displays synonyms (words with the same or very similar meaning) and antonyms (words with the opposite meaning) for the words you specify. To look up words with the Thesaurus, move the Insertion Point anywhere within the word you want to look up.

To open the Thesaurus:

- Click on the Thesaurus icon on the Power Bar, *or*
- Choose Tools and then Thesaurus.

The Thesaurus dialog box appears, as shown in Figure 9-3, with the current word highlighted and possible alternatives for that word listed in the first box.

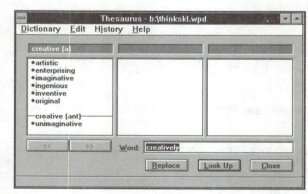

- Use the Scroll Bar to scroll through the list of alternatives.

Figure 9-3
Thesaurus dialog box

If you do not want to use any of the words that are displayed, you can have the Thesaurus suggest other alternatives by using *either* one of the following methods:

1. Double-click on a listed word that is marked with a bullet. The bullet indicates that there is a group of synonyms and antonyms available for that word. After you double-click on the word, the alternative words will appear in the next scroll box. A pointing hand icon appears to show you the path you are taking through the Thesaurus.

2. Key a word in the text box provided and then choose <u>L</u>ook Up.

- When you find the desired replacement, choose <u>R</u>eplace.

The exact word will be inserted, so you may need to add word endings such as "ed" or "ing" to the word.

▶ EXERCISE 9-6

1. Open the file named **thinkskl**.

2. Use the Thesaurus to look at each of the following words: `creatively`, `visualizes`, `constraints`, `alternatives`, and `relationship`. Use the Scroll Bar to look at these words, choose some of the words, and generally become familiar with the use of the Thesaurus. You will see the abbreviation "n" after the word "relationship," which indicates that the suggestions displayed in the scroll box are nouns. Other abbreviations are "v" for verb, "a" for adjective or adverb, and "ant" for antonym.

3. Close the file without resaving it.

USING GRAMMATIK

Grammatik is a grammar checker that comes with WordPerfect 6.0 for Windows. Grammatik checks your document for correct grammar, style, punctuation, and word usage. Along with the Speller and Thesaurus, Grammatik is a useful tool that can find many typos and grammatical errors; however, none of these replace proofreading. After you use these tools, *always review and proofread your document carefully to catch any other errors.*

Grammatik can help you make your writing better; but, for one reason on another, you may not always want to change what is written. You will need to decide what you want to do.

◆ N O T E ◆

It is always a good idea to save your document before you start Grammatik. If you later decide not to keep any changes made by Grammatik, you are sure to have a copy of your original document

TO OPEN GRAMMATIK:

- Click on the Grammatik button on the Power Bar, *or*
- Choose <u>T</u>ools and then <u>G</u>rammatik.

The Grammatik dialog box, as shown in Figure 9-4 on the next page, will appear. The dialog box shows the current settings. By default, Grammatik is set to check the entire document for grammar, mechanics, style, and spelling errors, with a general writing style of standard formality.

- Choose a proofreading mode from the Options menu.

The proofreading modes are described below.

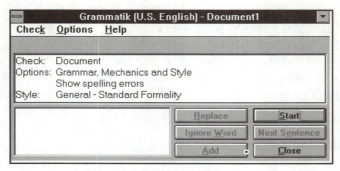

Figure 9-4
Grammatik dialog box

Proofreading Mode	Action Taken
Grammar, Mechanics, and Style	Uses grammatical, mechanical, and style rules to check your document.
Grammar and mechanics	Uses only grammatical and mechanical rules to proofread.
Statistics	Collects information about word and sentence structures, and then offers statistics on readability.

- Choose Start.

While Grammatik checks your document, the Grammatik window will display the errors it finds. Use the commands shown in Table 9-1 to respond to the errors Grammatik finds.

Command	Function
Replace	Replace the highlighted error with a new word. You can correct the problem manually if you do not agree with any of the suggestions. After a replacement is inserted, Grammatik goes to the next problem.
Skip	Ignore the highlighted error and go to the next detected error.
Next Sentence	Skip all remaining errors in the current sentence and go to the first problem in the next sentence.
Ignore Phrase Word	Ignore a specific word or phrase for the rest of the proofreading session, unless it is part of a grammar error.
Add	Add a word to the Grammatik user spelling dictionary.
Resume	Recheck from the current sentence onward.

You must save your document after you have run Grammatik on it. If you do not, all your changes will be lost.

Table 9-1

EXERCISE 9-7

1. Open **less1.** again. Click on the Grammatik icon on the Power Bar and then click on Start.

2. Grammatik will first highlight `had never been made` and tell you "This is passive voice. Consider revising, using active voice. See Help for more information." Move the Insertion Point to the beginning of the highlighted material and delete it; then insert `were not there`. Click on Resume.

3. Grammatik may display the message "Usually a paragraph should have more than one sentence." If so, ignore this by clicking on Skip because you know you started a new subject in the next paragraph.

4. Grammatik suggests trying a comma after `works`. Ignore this by clicking on Skip because a comma obviously does not make the sentence clearer.

5. Click on Skip on the next item because `print` is not plural as used.

6. Click on Skip because you want to keep the sentence as is, including `are listed`.

7. Grammatik tells you that `Several of the` is wordy. You decide to delete `Several of the` and begin the sentence with `More`. Click on Resume.

8. Change `don't` to `do not` and click on Resume.

9. When you are asked if you want to close Grammatik, choose No. The opening screen will again appear. This time choose Options, Statistics, and Start and the Document Statistics box shown in Figure 9-5 will appear.

10. Look at some of the things you can learn here, such as the word count, sentences per paragraph, words per sentence, and readability level. When you are through, Close both the Document Statistics box and Grammatik.

11. Save your revised document as **less1.grm.** Print this revised document and then Close it.

Figure 9-5
Document Statistics box

DOCUMENT INFORMATION

Sometimes you may want information about your document, but you do not want to go through Grammatik to obtain it. You can obtain some information if you:

- Choose File, and then Document Info.

As you will note in the Document Information box shown in Figure 9-6, the information provided is somewhat different from that in the Document Statistics box in Grammatik. When you are finished looking at the information, choose OK to close the Document Information box.

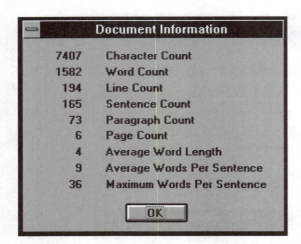

Figure 9-6
Document Information box

REVIEW

TRUE/FALSE

Circle the correct answer.

1. T F When you create footnotes, WordPerfect automatically numbers them, places them at the bottom of the appropriate page, and adjusts the page length accordingly.

2. T F WordPerfect will automatically renumber and reformat all footnotes or endnotes if you add or delete footnotes and endnotes.

3. T F All footnotes and endnotes are created at the end of the document and will be placed in the appropriate place by WordPerfect.

4. T F If you find an error in either a footnote or endnote, you should recreate it.

5. T F You should always correct the errors identified by Grammatik.

6. T F When a listed word in the Thesaurus is marked with a bullet, it indicates that the suggestions are nouns.

COMPLETION

Fill in the blank.

1. _____ _____ provide easy access to options related to a specific feature.

2. Footnotes are separated from the regular text with a _____ horizontal line.

3. If you put a title page at the end of a multi-page document, you will need to _____ any page numbering or headers and footers on it.

4. The WordPerfect _____ searches for and displays synonyms and antonyms for the words you specify.

5. If you insert a hard page break, the code you will see when you are in Reveal Codes is _____.

6. To obtain the word count of your document most rapidly, choose File and then _____ _____.

LESSON 9 FOOTNOTES, ENDNOTES, THESAURUS, AND GRAMMATIK

Troubleshooting with Reveal Codes: You wish to begin a new page at the end of the document for the endnotes, but the endnotes appear at the end of the last page. When you look at the expanded Endnote code in Reveal Codes, you see:

Open Style Endnote: Und`Ibid`**Und., **`pp. 11-`**Hyphen**`13`**HRt**

HRt

HRt

Hard Center on Margin`Endnotes`**HRt**

Why do the endnotes appear at the end of the last page rather than on a separate page?

REVIEW EXERCISE

The following exercise gives you practice in applying many of the WordPerfect 6.0 for Windows features which you have learned in past lessons. Try to insert the proper commands and codes and perform the directed actions without referring back to the lessons. If, however, you are not sure how to perform a function, look it up and study it carefully so that you will know how to do it in the future.

▶ **REVIEW EXERCISE 9-1**

1. Key the multi-page document shown in Figure 9-7 starting on the next page. Do <u>NOT</u> key the footnotes.
2. Save the base document (before revisions) with the name **security.1**.
3. Now go back and, using the Footnote feature, insert the three foot notes shown in Figure 9-7. The footnotes are shown at the end of the document.
4. Set line spacing to **2.0,** with a quadruple space following the title. Set the left margin at **1.5"**, with all other margins at **1"**. Left justify the text.
5. The title should be all in uppercase about 2" from the top of the paper. (Don't change the top margin setting. Instead, use **Enter** to add blank lines.)
6. Give the document a header as follows:

SYSTEMS SECURITY   Insert Page no.   Current Date

7. Suppress the header on the first page.
8. Turn on Widow/Orphan protection.
9. On the last line of the document, key the total number of words flush right.
10. Indent each new paragraph with a tab. Single-space and double indent each quotation.
11. Prepare a title page as part of the document, including the title of the document, your name, your instructor's name, and the date. Suppress the header on this page.
12. Spell-check and view the document to make sure everything is correct before printing.
13. Save the document as **security.rev** so you can differentiate the revised document from the original document. Print one copy and Close the file.

Systems Security

Information routinely crosses from personal computers into corporate databases and around the world through wide area networks and satellite communications. The number of people having direct access to computers has grown from 50 million to over 350 million worldwide today. By the year 2000, the worldwide PC computer population will reach into the billions. Even more important than the sheer number of computers or computer users are the ways in which we employ computers.

Before the age of office automation, the principal users of computer systems were data processing professionals. The two chief dangers were novices outside the organization breaking into the system or theft of funds or data by employees. The proliferation of computers throughout an organization has extended accessibility and vulnerability to noncomputer professionals. Traditionally, data processing professionals were informed and educated about the legal and ethical obligations of protecting confidentiality and assuring data security. Now every user should be aware of the dangers.

Security involves hardware, software, and networks. Security is defined as the protection against accidental or intentional theft, modification, or destruction of information and data.[1]

In addition, security is concerned with the protection of confidentiality and the privacy of individuals and entities about whom information is stored. Security is also concerned with acts of computer crimes which have bases of information, bulletin boards, and corporate mainframes. Finally, security is related to the professional ethics of programmers and end users of software.

Other related issues include identifying the symptoms of security problems, understanding the ways that loss of data can occur, being aware of the damaging impact of viruses, and knowing which precautions to take to avoid breaches of security.

"In computing, managing distributed microcomputers to improve productivity and to secure them against viruses and other malicious software necessitates the implementation of the combination of software execution control and software quality assurance."[2]

A virus is one of the most dangerous forms of sabotage. A virus is a program introduced without permission or knowledge of management. The distinguishing feature of a virus is that it attaches itself to another program and reproduces itself. The name is derived from its similarity to the way a human disease virus infects a cell and is reproduced when the cell reproduces.

A computer virus can be benign (harmless), in which case it may only display a "have a nice day" message. Other viruses, however, are definitely cancerous. Since the virus makes copies of itself, when you discover it in one place, you must check everywhere to be sure you are rid of it. A virus may lie dormant for a time or merely reproduce for a while before activating its destructive purpose. It can spread through multiple systems and will attach itself to every system which it touches.

"Experts estimate that computer crime costs the U.S. economy upward to $50 billion annually. These are typically 'perfect crimes' in the sense that detection is difficult and only one out of every 22,000 computer crimes results in a conviction. Winn Schwartau, Executive Director of the International Partnership Against Computer Terrorism, believes that an estimated 521 viruses have been identified and that an average of 12 new computer viruses are being introduced every day."[3]

Other factors that contribute to compromising computer security include: the spread of electronic mail systems; the ability to upload or download data to and from a host (mainframe) by anyone with access to a computer facility, terminal, and magnetic disks or tapes; and the interconnection of personal computers without systems controls that allow individuals to exchange data.

Without centralized auditing and systems controls, data becomes more accessible to computer-literate users as well as to hackers (unauthorized people who find a way to enter a system) invading the corporate and individual privacy of others.

Large databases about individuals at one time were primarily concentrated in the government and in financial institutions. Even then it was difficult to acquire and maintain the volume of personal information stored in computers. Access was highly

centralized and controlled. Now it is no longer true
that gathering of personal data is confined to such
databases. Nor is it true that the same centralized
level of control is consistently applied. Mailing
lists are traded, rented, and sold to hundreds of
organizations.

Corporations maintain personal databases about
individuals in human resource files. The Internal
Revenue service, therefore the federal government, now
has financial histories about everyone who has ever
filed. Income tax returns have been maintained on file
for years and are cross referenced with judicial and
law enforcement systems. Data about one person in the
United States can be stored in many computers in the
U.S., as well as worldwide. The public is becoming
more and more aware that computer systems can and do
allow invasion of privacy, and they are seeking
protective measures.

(Here are the footnotes for you to insert at the proper locations in the text.)

[1]Kathleen P. Wagoner and Mary M. Ruprecht, END-USER COMPUTING, South-Western Publishing Company, 1993, p. 270.

[2]Peter S. Tippett, PhD., M.D., Case Western Reserve University, Cleveland, Ohio; and President, Certus International, Cleveland, Ohio.

[3]Kathleen P. Wagoner and Mary M. Ruprecht, MANUAL FOR END-USER COMPUTING, South-Western Publishing Company, 1993, p. 10.

Figure 9-7

LESSON 10

Multiple Windows/Multiple Documents

OBJECTIVES

Upon completion of this lesson, you will be able to:
1. Open more than one document.
2. View multiple windows.
3. Switch among document windows.
4. Cut, copy, and paste between document windows.
5. Close a document window and all documents.

WordPerfect 6.0 for Windows provides the capability of using several documents at one time. The benefits are numerous. You can edit more than one document, switching instantly from one to another. You can copy and move text between documents, and you can have other documents readily available for reference. You can have one activity being performed in one window (such as printing) while working in another window. In fact, if you have plenty of memory in your computer, you can have up to nine documents open at the same time.

OPENING MORE THAN ONE DOCUMENT

You can use either the New or Open command on the File menu to open another document window. The **New** command opens a new and empty document window so that you can create a new document. When you use the **Open** command, WordPerfect opens another window and prompts you to open a document already saved to disk.

To view the list of all currently open files, activate the Window menu by choosing Window. In the example shown in Figure 10-1, there are three windows open. The check mark next to the third document indicates that this is the one that is currently active (contains the Insertion Point). To make one of the other documents in this list active, simply select it from the list.

If you try to open more than one copy of the same document, you will see a message telling you that the document is in use. You are told that if you edit the document, you must save it with a new name. You can then decide whether to continue by choosing Yes or No.

Figure 10-1
Three windows are open, with the Insertion Point in the third document

In this exercise, you will learn how to work with multiple documents and multiple windows. Follow the directions given in numbered steps below.

▶ **EXERCISE 10-1**

1. To create your first window, Open the existing document named **less1**.

2. With **less1** still on the screen, Open the existing document named **keyboard**.

3. With **keyboard** still on the screen, Open the existing document named **document**.

4. Choose Window to view the list of documents.

VIEWING MULTIPLE WINDOWS

WordPerfect provides you with two ways of quickly arranging multiple windows on the screen. After choosing Window, you can choose the Cascade option so that windows are overlapped and you can see only the Title Bar of the other windows. Or you can choose Tile to arrange windows so that each window takes up a portion of the screen, with no window overlapping another window.

Try these steps to see how you can Tile or Cascade the document windows in WordPerfect.

1. Choose Window and then Cascade. All three windows are reduced in size, with the current document (the one you are working on) on top, as shown in Figure 10-2. Click on one of the document windows in the back to make that document window the currently active one.

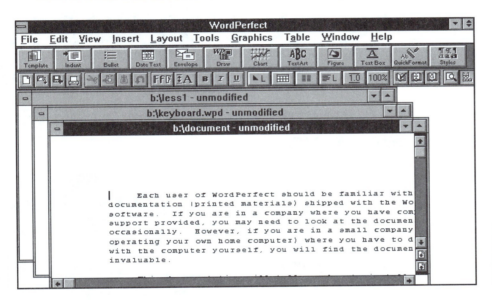

Figure 10-2
Cascade option showing the three documents that are open.

2. Choose Window and then Tile. One window is displayed above the other as shown in Figure 10-3 on the next page. Again, simply clicking on a document window will make this document the active one, denoted by a highlighted Title Bar. Any commands you select from the Menu Bar at the top of the screen will affect the active document.

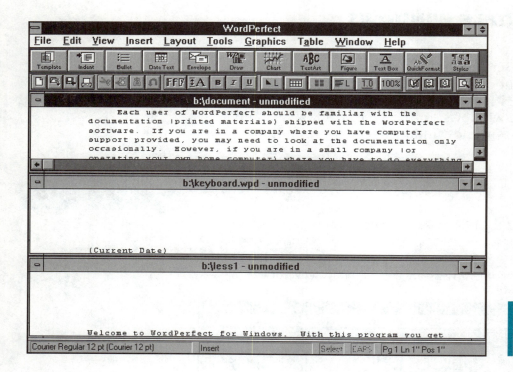

Figure 10-3
Tile option showing the three documents that are open.

SWITCHING BETWEEN DOCUMENTS

If you are displaying more than one document at once with either the Tile or Cascade option, switching between documents is as easy as clicking anywhere in the other document's window.

If one document is maximized (taking up all available space on the screen and obscuring the other document windows), you will need to switch between documents with the Window menu.

To use the Window menu:

- Choose Window from the Menu Bar.

You will see a list of currently open files. (See Figure 10-1.) Remember, the check mark indicates the document that is currently active.

- Choose the document you want by clicking on the file name or by typing the number assigned to the document in the Window menu. The document window will now contain the file you selected.

Only one Status Bar is displayed at the bottom of the screen, regardless of how many documents are open. The Status Bar shows the Insertion Point location and font for the current document only. This is also true for the Ruler Bar, if you are using it.

Try switching between documents:

1. Move the mouse pointer to an inactive document (i.e., **keyboard**) and click. Notice the change in the Title Bar and sizing buttons.

2. Click on the Maximize button in the upper right corner of the document window (the button with a triangle pointing upward). The document window now takes up all the available work space on the screen.

3. Choose Window from the Menu Bar. You will see the list shown earlier in Figure 10-1.

4. Choose the document you want by clicking on the file name (i.e., **less1**). The document window should now contain the file you selected (i.e., **less1**).

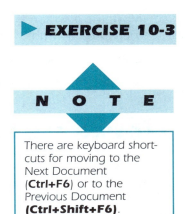

NOTE: There are keyboard shortcuts for moving to the Next Document (**Ctrl+F6**) or to the Previous Document (**Ctrl+Shift+F6**).

CUTTING, COPYING, AND PASTING BETWEEN DOCUMENTS

In Lesson 6, you learned how to move text from one location in a document to another by Cutting or Copying and Pasting. You can just as easily move text between documents. This is especially easy when you have both the documents displayed on the screen, since you can see the Cut-and-Paste operation happening.

Remember, the Cut or Copy command sends text to a holding place called the Clipboard. The text can then be pasted into another location in the same document, in a different document, or even in another Windows application.

CLOSING A DOCUMENT WINDOW

When you are finished with a document, you should close the document window with the Close command on the File menu. If you have not saved the document (or any changes that were made to the document), you are asked if you want to save the document (or changes to the document) before WordPerfect closes the window.

By performing the following steps, you can both review Copy and Paste and copy text from one document to another.

1. Click in the **keyboard** document to make it the active window.

2. Scroll to the second paragraph and Select the paragraph which begins `CUA stands for Common User Access`.

3. Choose Edit and then Copy.

4. Click in the **less1** document.

5. Move the Insertion Point to a point a double space below the end of the last paragraph.
6. Choose Edit and then Paste. Adjust the spacing, if necessary.
7. Save the file as **keyboard.1** and Close the document.

CLOSING ALL DOCUMENTS

If you want to close all the documents and the WordPerfect application at once, you can use the Exit command on the File menu instead. Before exiting, you are also asked if you want to save the documents (or any changes to the documents) if you have not already done so.

You still have the **less1** document open in your first document window and the **document** file open in the second window. Select the first paragraph from the text named **document**, copy the selected text, and paste it into **less1** to appear as the last paragraph of that document. Adjust the spacing, if necessary, and Save this new document with the name **less10**. Print a copy and Close all documents by Exiting WordPerfect.

REVIEW

TRUE/FALSE

Circle the correct answer.

1. T   F   WordPerfect 6.0 for Windows provides the capability of using several documents at one time.

2. T   F   Although you can edit more than one document at a time by switching from one to another, you cannot choose a command to print all documents that are open.

3. T   F   The New command opens a new and empty document window so that you can create a new document.

4. T   F   Only the Status Bar for the current document is displayed at the bottom of the screen, regardless of how many documents are open.

5. T   F   The Status Bar shows the current location and font for the current document only.

6. T   F   You can use Cut, Copy, and Paste between documents as well as within a document.

COMPLETION

Fill in the blank.

1. If you have enough memory, you can have up to _____ documents open at the same time.

2. To open another document window, you can use either the _____ or _____ command.

3. To view the list of all currently open files, you should open the _____ menu.

4. WordPerfect provides two ways of arranging multiple windows on the screen. After choosing Window, you can choose the _____ option or the _____ option.

5. If you want to close all the documents and the WordPerfect application at once, choose File and then the _____ command.

Troubleshooting with Reveal Codes: You have copied and pasted a double-spaced paragraph from the middle of a document in one window to a document in another. You discover that it is single-spaced. Why would this occur?

LESSON 11

Managing Files

OBJECTIVES:

Upon completion of this lesson, you will be able to:

1. Understand the information on your files that is available to you on the Open File, Insert File, and Save As dialog boxes.
2. Use the various commands available to you through the File Options and QuickMenu drop-down menus to manage your files.
3. View a file without opening it.
4. Use various File options.
5. Use QuickFinder.
6. Use QuickList.

When you start using WordPerfect 6.0 for Windows, you will have only a few documents stored on a disk. Managing them should not be too difficult because you will remember their contents and perhaps their file names. As you create more and more documents, however, managing them becomes more important.

In WordPerfect 6.0 for Windows, file management capabilities are provided any time there is a file listing on a dialog box, such as when you use Open File, Insert File, and Save As. Through these dialog boxes, WordPerfect makes it possible to name, find, view, copy, move, rename, print, and delete files.

OPEN FILE

You will find the Open File dialog box easy to use to manage your files. To begin:

- Choose File and then Open, *or* click on the Open button on the Power Bar.

The Open File dialog box will appear. (See Figure 11-1.)

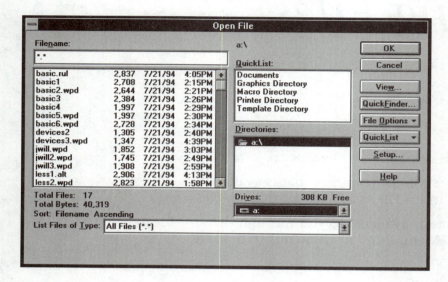

Figure 11-1
Open File dialog box

FILENAME

The Filename box appears at the top of the dialog box, with a list of files from the default directory displayed below in the list box. The Filename box displays *.*, which means that all of the files in the directory are listed.

To open a particular file, highlight the name of the file, and then double-click or choose OK to open the file.

Below the Filename list, you will also see that WordPerfect tells you the total number of files and the total bytes which they take. You can also learn the number of kilobytes free on the drive which has been selected.

LIST FILES OF TYPE

If you have many files in one directory and you don't want to search them all to find your file, click on the arrow on the right side of the List Files of Type box. (See Figure 11-2.) A drop-down menu will appear, listing different kinds of files from which you can select. Once a file type is selected, only files with that extension are displayed in the Filename list box. This is only helpful if you have given your files the specified extension. To display only the files that have one of your own special extensions, delete the second asterisk in the Filename text box and key your own extension (for example, *.mem for all your memo files).

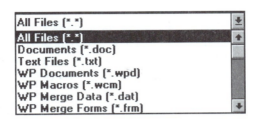

Figure 11-2
List Files of Type box

CHANGING DIRECTORIES AND DRIVES

The Directories list box lets you view a list of directories in a selected drive. You can easily change drives by clicking on the arrow on the right side of the Drives box and choosing the drive you want. If you want to open a directory, double-click the directory name in the directories list. The files in that directory will then be listed in the Filename list box. Any subdirectories will be listed beneath the directory you just opened.

INFORMATION ON FILES

You can see the number of existing files, the number of bytes in those files, and the number of bytes free or available on the drive or disk; that is, the amount of empty space remaining on the drive or disk.

A double-density 3.5" disk holds 720K (roughly 720,000 bytes), while a high-density disk holds 1.44Mb (1,440,000 bytes) of information. You should not use more than 75 to 80 percent of the available disk space so that you have the flexibility to revise the documents already saved. In addition, the computer's operating system limits you to 112 files in the first-level (root) directory on a double-density disk and 224 files on a high-density disk. When you reach that limit, even if you have enough bytes free, you will receive an error message and cannot continue.

Therefore, the information WordPerfect gives you is very important. If your disk is getting too full, you can delete some of the documents you no longer need or move them into a subdirectory.

VIEWING A FILE

Once you have highlighted a file from the file list, you can look at the file without opening if you:

- Click on View.

The file will appear in a box in the lower right-hand corner. Although it will not be WYSIWYG, you can easily identify whether a particular file is what you want without having to open it.

To view a file:

1. With the Open File dialog box on your screen, highlight any file you want by clicking on it once.
2. Click on View and note the appearance of the file.
3. Close the Viewer by double-clicking on the control menu box in the upper left corner of the Viewer window.

▶ **EXERCISE 11-1**

USING THE FILE OPTIONS

By clicking on the File Options button on the right side of the Open File dialog box, you will see the list of functions shown in Figure 11-3. WordPerfect makes it possible for you to perform these file management activities quickly and easily. You can also obtain the same features by placing the mouse pointer anywhere in the Filename list box and clicking on the right mouse button to display the QuickMenu.

```
Copy...
Move...
Rename...
Delete...
Change Attributes...
Print...
Print File List...
Create Directory...
Remove Directory...
```

Figure 11-3
File Options menu

PRINT FILE

Instead of opening a file to print it, you can print it directly from the Open File dialog box, through either the File Options or QuickMenu drop-down menus.

- Click on Print and the Print File dialog box shown in Figure 11-4 on the next page, will appear.

Figure 11-4
Print File dialog box

If you have already highlighted a file, that name will appear in the dialog box; or you can key the file name and press **Enter.** This is much faster than displaying the document on the screen, sending it to the printer, and then closing the document.

Now Print a file directly from the screen.

▶ **EXERCISE 11-2**

1. With the Open File dialog box on your screen, highlight **keyboard.1**.
2. Click on the File Options button and then on Print on the drop-down menu. The Print File dialog box will appear. Since you have already highlighted **keyboard.1,** that name will appear in the dialog box; all you have to do is press **Enter.**
3. Cancel out of the Open File dialog box.

DELETING FILES

You can delete documents very easily using either the File Options or QuickMenu drop-down menus, but *be careful!* Delete a document only if you are *sure* you will never want the document again. Once a document is deleted, you cannot undelete it without using another kind of software. Before you delete a file, you should first double-check the contents.

When you have created several different versions of a file, you will sometimes want to clean up your disk and delete all but the latest version. This not only saves disk space, but also saves possible confusion later about which version was the final draft.

When deleting, always proceed carefully. Check and double-check the file you want to delete to make sure you will never again want the document.

- Click on Delete and the Delete File dialog box shown in Figure 11-5 will appear.

Figure 11-5
Delete File dialog box

If you have already highlighted a file, that name will appear in the dialog box; or you can key the file name. Make sure the file name is correct, and then click on Delete or press **Enter.** There is no warning message giving you a chance to change your mind.

When several files are listed in a row, you can highlight more than one at a time by clicking on the first one and holding down the left mouse button and dragging the mouse pointer down to highlight a series of file names. Or you can hold down the **Ctrl** key and click the mouse pointer on non-consecutive files to select them.

▶ **EXERCISE 11-3**

You will no longer use the following files, so you can Delete them now, using a combination of the methods you learned previously: **basic1, basic2, basic3, basic4, basic5, basic.rul, jwill1, jwill2, jwill3, food1, food2, paydue, fonts1, fonts2, membcom.let, membcom.rev, keyboard and keyboard1., less1.alt, less1.rev, less2.rev, phone,** *and* **recycle3.**

RENAMING FILES

Renaming files is a very useful way in which to reorganize and manage your files better. When you Rename a file, the document file appears under a new file name, and the old file name no longer exists. The Renaming function is also performed through the File Options or QuickMenu drop-down menus.

- Click on <u>R</u>ename and the Rename File dialog box shown in Figure 11-6 will appear.

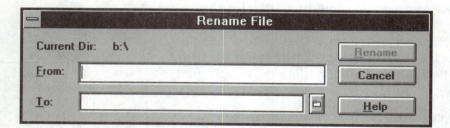

Figure 11-6
Rename File dialog box

If you have already highlighted a file, that name will appear in the dialog box. Be sure it is the file you want and then key in the To box the new name under which you want this file to appear. Then click on <u>R</u>ename or press **Enter**.

Rename the file named **devices3** *to* **devices.fnl.**

▶ **EXERCISE 11-4**

COPYING A DOCUMENT

Copying a document works in a similar fashion to renaming, except that the original version of the file is maintained in its original place. A common use for copying documents is to create backup copies to avoid loss in case a document becomes damaged or lost. One way to make a copy of a document is to save it under another name or to another disk.

Before copying, it is a good idea to look at the information available to you to see how much space is left on the floppy disk that you are planning to copy files onto. The major benefit of copying through File Options or the QuickMenu is that you can copy a file on disk instead of having to open it into a window, resave it, and close it.

The copying function is also performed through the File Options or QuickMenu drop-down menus.

- Click on Copy and the Copy File dialog box shown in Figure 11-7 will appear.
- Key the path or file name you want the file copied to and click on Copy.

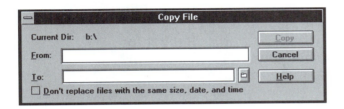

Figure 11-7
Copy File dialog box

You can click on the list button to select a directory. Also, you can choose the drive you want to copy the file to. Then choose OK.

*If you have access to another disk, Copy **suller.let** there now.*

▶ **EXERCISE 11-5**

You can select all files in the Filename list box by placing the Insertion Point on any file in the box and pressing **Ctrl** and the slash key **(/)**. This is especially useful when you want to copy an entire disk.

PRINT FILE LIST

There are times when it is convenient to have a hard copy of the files listed in the Open File dialog box directory. You can obtain a copy that will match the information displayed in the file list by using Print File List.

Using either the File Options or QuickMenu drop-down menus:

- Click on Print File List and the Print File List dialog box shown in Figure 11-8 will appear.

Figure 11-8
Print File List dialog box

LESSON 11   MANAGING FILES   **WP143**

You can select or highlight a series of the files by clicking on one and dragging the mouse pointer down over the series of files you wish to print. Then click on Print List of Selected Files. Or you can click on Print Entire List if you want the entire list to be printed, and then click on Print.

In this exercise, Print a list of your files.

▶ **EXERCISE 11-6**

QUICKFINDER

In the Open File dialog box, you can click on the QuickFinder button and then see the dialog box shown in Figure 11-9. Using **QuickFinder,** you can search for files by file pattern, words or phrases, a date range, etc. For example, assume that you want to search for all your documents written to Habitat for Humanity between 1/3/94 and 2/6/94. You know that the words "Habitat for Humanity" are written in every letter, but you can't remember the file name given to any of them. QuickFinder will find these documents for you.

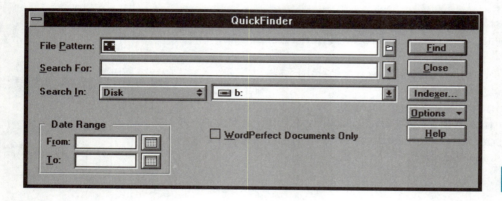

Figure 11-9
Quick Finder dialog box

In this exercise, you will learn to use QuickFinder to search for some words and phrases in YOUR files.

▶ **EXERCISE 11-7**

1. With the Open File dialog box on the screen, choose QuickFinder and the QuickFinder dialog box will appear.

2. Move to the File Pattern text box and click on the button at the right of the text box to select the directory you want to search. The Select Directory dialog box shown in Figure 11-10 will appear. In this case, THE DIRECTORY FOR YOUR STORAGE DISK SHOULD BE THE DEFAULT. If not, key it or select the proper drive. Click on OK.

WP144 LESSON 11 MANAGING FILES

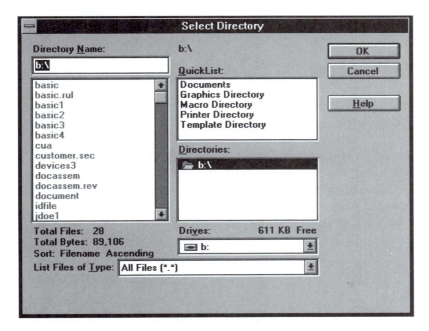

Figure 11-10
Select Directory dialog box

3. Move to the Search For text box and key security.

4. If you don't have any idea as to the file's location, click on the arrows at the right of Search In:, and then choose Directory.

5. Move down to the Date Range group of boxes. In the From text box, key a date two months ago (in this format: mm/dd/yy). In the To text box, key today as the ending date or click on the calendar icon and click on Today (to enter today's date).

6. Now choose Find and the Searching box will appear. (See Figure 11-11.) You can see the file names appear as they are searched. Finally, the name(s) of files in which security appears will be shown in the Search Results list. You can then go to the file(s) listed to find the particular document you want.

7. Now follow the same procedure to search for the phrase basic skills. This time, Print a list of the files in which this phrase appears. In the Search Results List dialog box, choose File Options and then Print List. Notice that you can do this directly from the Search Results dialog box. Then Close the Search Results list and Cancel the Open File dialog box.

Figure 11-11
Searching box

LESSON 11   MANAGING FILES   **WP145**

For more information on QuickFinder, see the WordPerfect 6.0 for Windows Reference Manual or User's Guide.

QUICKLIST

A **QuickList** contains files and directories you use most. You can access a particular file or directory much more quickly than by keying its name or searching through the entire disk directory. To add an item that you may use frequently, choose QuickList, and then choose Add Item. (You can also click the right mouse button over the QuickList, and then choose Add Item.) Key a file name in the Description text box and choose OK to add the item to your QuickList.

From then on, all you do is double-click on the entry that you want in the QuickList and that file or directory will be immediately opened for you to work in.

As you have learned, there are many functions you can perform by working through the Open File, Insert File, and Save As dialog boxes. All of them can help you do a better job of managing files. These functions are especially valuable because you can access considerable information through these dialog boxes, and you can perform such functions as copying and deleting without having to exit to the operating system to perform them.

REVIEW

TRUE/FALSE

Circle the correct answer.

1. T F To perform most document management activities, you will need to exit to your operating system.

2. T F You can view, open, copy, move, rename, print, or delete through the Save As dialog box.

3. T F On a dialog box which lists files, you can also see the number of existing files, the number of bytes in those files, and the number of bytes free or available on the drive or disk.

4. T F If you accidentally delete a document, you can use WordPerfect's Undelete command to restore it, if you do so immediately.

5. T F You can print directly through the Open File dialog box without opening the file.

6. T F You can obtain a copy of the information displayed in the file list by using Print File List.

COMPLETION

Fill in the blank.

1. You should not use more than _____ to _____ of the available space on a disk or a drive so that you have the flexibility to revise the documents already saved.

2. Through _____, you can see a portion of the contents of a particular file.

3. A common use for copying is to create _____ copies to avoid loss in case a document becomes damaged or lost.

4. When you _____ a file, the old file name is removed and the document appears under a new file name.

5. Using _____, you can search for files by file pattern, words or phrases, a date range, etc.

6. The files and directories you use most can be displayed with a _____.

Troubleshooting: When working in WordPerfect, what is the easiest and quickest way for you to find out how many bytes are free on your disk and the number of files you have on disk?

LESSON 12

Tables

OBJECTIVES

Upon completion of this lesson, you will be able to:

1. Create a table.
2. Edit the table structure.
3. Add text and calculate totals.
4. Delete a table.

The Tables feature helps you to quickly and easily organize information into rows and columns without using tabs or tab settings. Graphics lines divide a table into boxes, known as cells, which can hold text, numbers, or formulas.

CREATING TABLES

To create a table:

- Choose Table and then Create.

The Create Table dialog box will appear, as shown in Figure 12-1. You will then enter the number of columns and rows.

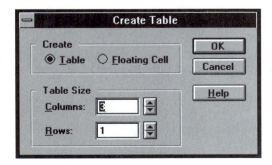

Figure 12-1
Create Table dialog box

WP149

A faster way to create a table is to click on the Table Quick Create button on the Power Bar and drag the mouse pointer down until you have highlighted the number of rows and cells you need in your table. When you release the mouse button, the table you have defined will appear.

Throughout this lesson, you are to perform a series of exercises in which you will learn to create a table and enter text in a table that will be a basic invoice as shown in Figure 12-2. Follow along carefully. Do *not* key the contents until you are told to do so.

Kay's Catering	
Description	Totals
4 gal. Sweet Punch	$10.00
12 doz. Assorted Cookies	$18.00
1 Vegetable Tray with Dip	$16.50
Please Pay This Amount	$44.50

▌ Figure 12-2

▶ **EXERCISE 12-1**

Let's create a table through the menus:

1. Choose Table and then Create and the Create Table dialog box will appear.

2. Enter the number of columns (you can key up to 32). In this case, click on the arrows until you obtain 2, OR key 2 and press **Tab.**

3. Key the number of rows; in this case, 6.

4. Choose OK and the table will appear at the Insertion Point. This table should look just like Figure 12-3.

5. Save the table with the name **table1** and close the file.

▌ Figure 12-3

Now try using the Power Bar method:

1. Place the Insertion Point where you want the table to appear.
2. Click and hold on the Table Quick Create button on the Power Bar.
3. Drag the pointer until you have defined a table with two columns and six rows.
4. Release the mouse button and the table will appear at the Insertion Point. This table also should look just like Figure 12-3.
5. Save the table with the name **table2** and Close the file.

Which method do you think is easiest and fastest? From now on, you can use either the Table menu or the Power Bar button, whichever you prefer, to create a table.

STATUS BAR

When the Insertion Point is inside a table, the Status Bar at the bottom of the document window shows the address of the cell where the Insertion Point is currently located; in this case, in Table A, Cell A1. Table A means you are in the first table in the document. (Table C would refer to the third table in the document.) Columns are lettered and rows are numbered, so Cell A1 means you are in the first column (A) and the first row (1).

USING REVEAL CODES

If you look in Reveal Codes, you will see a Table Definition code **[Tbl Def]** at the beginning of the table. This is an expandable code because when you click on it, it will expand to **[Tbl Def:TABLE A; 3.25", 3.25"]**, where A is a letter that represents the table number in a document, and 3.25" represents the different widths for each column.

You will also see the codes **[Row]** and **[Cell]** wherever there is a new row or cell. For example, since you just created a table consisting of six rows of two cells apiece, you would see in Reveal Codes, **[Row] [Cell]** repeated six times. At the end of the table, you will see the code **[Tbl Off]**.

EDITING THE TABLE STRUCTURE

Once you have created a table, you can change its structure. For example, you can join or split cells and insert rows or columns. To edit a table's structure, you must place the Insertion Point inside a table *or* Select the table.

SELECTING CELLS TO BE FORMATTED OR EDITED

Before you learn about formatting text and editing the table structure, you need to learn how to Select the cells, rows, or columns that are to be affected. Only the cells that are to be formatted or edited should be Selected. When you move the mouse pointer near the top border of a cell, notice how it changes to an arrow pointing up. When you move the mouse pointer near the left border of a cell, notice that it changes to an arrow pointing left. After you see the arrow, you can do the following to Select the current cell, a row, a column, or the entire table using the mouse.

Item to be Selected	Steps
Cell	Display either arrow and click once.
Row	Display the left arrow and double-click.
Column	Display the up arrow and double-click.
Entire table	Display either arrow and triple-click.

To Select (highlight) several cells, rows, or columns, display either arrow in a top or corner cell of the cells to be selected and drag the mouse through the table to the end or opposite corner of the group to be selected. To deselect the highlighted cells, click anywhere inside or outside the table.

BUTTON BAR

A fast way to work with tables is to use the Tables Button Bar that comes with WordPerfect 6.0 for Windows. The Tables Button Bar should be visible any time your Insertion Point is located within a table. If the Tables Button Bar, shown in Figure 12-4, isn't already showing, place the mouse pointer anywhere on the Button Bar, click the right mouse button, and select Tables from the list of available Button Bars.

Figure 12-4
Tables Button Bar

Another easy way to work faster with tables is to use the QuickMenus built into the Tables feature. We will use both QuickMenus and the Button Bar in the following exercises so that you can become familiar with both. Many of the features on the Tables Button Bar are also available in the QuickMenus.

JOINING CELLS

Notice how quickly you can join cells in the following exercise using QuickMenu.

1. Open **table1**.
2. Place the mouse pointer at the far left side of Cell A1. When the left-pointing arrow appears, double-click. This Selects the first row.
3. Now right-click to bring up the QuickMenu.
4. Choose Join Cells.

▶ **EXERCISE 12-3**

JUSTIFICATION, ATTRIBUTES, AND SIZE

By using the Format Tbl button on the Button Bar, you can very easily access the Format dialog box shown in Figure 12-5. On just this one dialog box, you can very quickly set a number of attributes, such as bold, italic, etc., and change the point size too. This, of course, is much quicker than setting each of them one at a time.

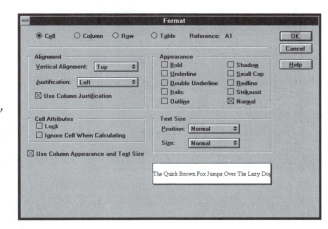

Figure 12-5
Format dialog box

Because the formatting of the first two rows is slightly different, we will do them one at a time.

▶ **EXERCISE 12-4**

1. Place the Insertion Point in Cell A1 and click the Format Tbl button on the Tables Feature Bar, OR right hyphen click to bring up the Quick Menu.
2. In the Alignment group box, set Justification to Center.
3. In the Appearance group box, select Bold.
4. In the Text Size group box, set Size to Very Large. You can see how each of the changes affects your text in the sample text box at the bottom of the dialog box. Choose OK to close the dialog box.
5. Move the Insertion Point to Cell A2. Select Row 2 by moving the Insertion Point to the left edge of the cell until the left-pointing arrow appears, and then double-click to highlight the row.
6. This time, right-click to open the QuickMenus and click on Format to open the Format dialog box. Because you have selected a row of the table, only the Row options will appear.
7. Select Cell to get the Cell options.

8. In the Alignment group box, choose Justification and select Center.

9. In the Appearance group box, select Bold.

10. Choose OK to close the dialog box.

SHADING/LINE STYLES

Cells can be shaded for added emphasis. You can use shading in titles or to highlight a certain column or row. The default for shading is 10% of black, with 100% being solid black.

You can access Lines/Fill either through QuickMenu *or* by choosing Table and then Lines/Fill. The Table Lines/Fill dialog box will appear. (See Figure 12-6.)

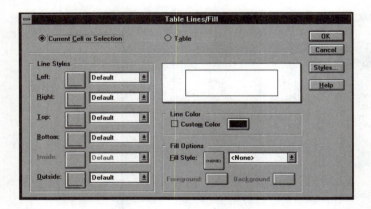

Figure 12-6
Table Lines/Fill dialog box

You have two ways to choose your line style and shading. In the Line Styles group box, each of the options, such as Top, Bottom, etc., has a large button. If you click the button, a **palette** (a box or window that contains available choices) of fill patterns will appear which will *show* you the various styles from which you can choose. If you click on the arrow at the right of the box, a drop-down menu will appear which will *list* the names of the various styles from which you can choose.

EXERCISE 12-5

1. To shade the row and change its top line, be sure the second row is still Selected and right-click. Then choose Lines/Fill from the QuickMenu. Experiment with choosing the following style. Click on the large buttons to see how the choices look and click on the down arrow to see a drop-down list of the choices.

2. Change the Top option to Double.

3. Change the Fill Style option to 10% Fill.

4. Choose OK to close the dialog box.

To shade the last row:

5. Select Row 6 by moving the Insertion Point to the left edge of Cell A6 until the left-pointing arrow appears and double-clicking.

6. Now right-click to open the QuickMenus and click on Format to open the Format dialog box.

7. Select the Cell button at the top of the dialog box.

8. In the Appearance group box, select Bold.

9. Choose OK.

10. Now shade the last row of the table with a 10% Fill and change its top line to Double (refer to the previous directions if you do not remember how to do this). Choose OK. Click anywhere in the table to deselect the row.

CHANGING COLUMN WIDTHS

You can change the width of each column by moving the mouse pointer to the line dividing the column and dragging the line to a new location. Or you can set exact measurements through the Format dialog box.

The first column needs to be wider than the second column. Therefore:

▶ **EXERCISE 12-6**

1. Place the Insertion Point in the first column and bring up the Format dialog box (either through QuickMenu or through the Table menu).

2. Select Column to display the column settings. The Column Width group box is located at the bottom of the dialog box. Move the Insertion Point to the Width box, key 5.0", and then choose OK to close the dialog box.

CHANGING JUSTIFICATION OPTIONS

Text is aligned (justified) at the left edge of a cell by default. You can change the justification through the Format dialog box so that text is aligned at the right, centered, or aligned on a decimal point (useful for columns of numbers). You can also choose Full justification, aligning the text at both the left and right sides of a cell. You can change the justification for an entire column or for a selected number of cells.

NUMBER TYPE

Through the Number Type dialog box, WordPerfect helps you to get the right type of number in a table. For example, you can choose Currency or Date/Type from the Available Types, according to what you plan for a column to contain. In the following exercise, you will learn how to use the Number Type dialog box to perform a number of steps.

You need to change the type of number in Column 2. Therefore:

1. To select cells B3 through B6, place the Insertion Point in B3, and then click and drag the mouse point to B6.

2. Click the Format Tbl button, and set the Justification to Decimal Align, and then choose OK.

3. Click the Table # Type button on the Button Bar; the Number Type dialog box shown in Figure 12-7 will appear.

4. In the Available Types group box, select Currency.

5. Choose OK.

6. Click in another part of the table to deselect the rows.

▶ **EXERCISE 12-7**

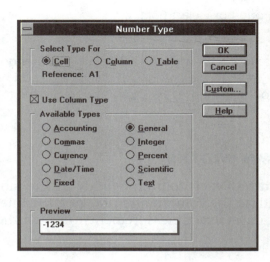

Figure 12-7
Number Type dialog box

ADDING TEXT AND CALCULATING TOTALS

Keying text in a table is just the same as keying text outside a table, except that some things will be done for you. For example, you do not enter the total because that can be calculated, nor do you need to key the dollar sign ($) because the column is already formatted for Currency and the dollar sign will be inserted automatically.

To move from cell to cell as you key, press **Tab** to move forward and **Shift+Tab** to move backward. You can also use **Alt+any arrow key** to move around in a table.

1. Key all of the text of the table shown in Figure 12-2, except the total in Cell B6. Remember to press **Tab** to move from cell to cell. The $ will automatically be inserted because the column is formatted for currency.

2. Place the Insertion Point in Cell B6.

3. Choose TblFormBar from the Button Bar. Note the Table Formula Feature Bar below the Power Bar or Ruler Bar, as shown in Figure 12-8.

▶ **EXERCISE 12-8**

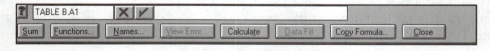

Figure 12-8
Table Formula Feature Bar

4. On the Feature Bar, click on Sum, which means "total all of the above numbers." The total of the cells will be inserted into Cell B6.

5. Choose Close to close the Table Formula Feature Bar.
6. Save this document as **invoice.12.** Print a copy and Close the file.

You have learned how to create a table invoice and change its appearance. In the next exercises, you will learn more ways in which WordPerfect helps you to handle tables. Follow along carefully as other changes are shown to you.

INSERTING ROWS OR COLUMNS

WordPerfect automatically inserts new rows or columns immediately *before* the row or column in which you place the Insertion Point. The new row or column will contain the same format settings as the row or column in which you place the Insertion Point.

To insert a row or column, place the Insertion Point where you want the new row or column to appear.

- Choose Insert from either the QuickMenu or the Table dropdown menu. The Insert Columns/Rows dialog box will appear.
- Key the number of columns or rows you want to insert in your table, and then choose OK.

If you want the new row or column placed *after* the row or column in which you place the Insertion Point, you must click on After.

To improve the appearance of the invoice, you decide to insert a blank row between the table title and the column titles.

▶ **EXERCISE 12-9**

1. Open the file named **invoice.12.**
2. To insert a row, place the Insertion Point in the second row.
3. Choose QuickMenu, and then choose Insert and Rows.
4. If necessary, key the number of rows (1) you want to insert in your table, and then choose OK.
5. Join the new row of cells as you did earlier in the exercises.
6. Save this file as **invoice.rev,** but do not Close the file.

DELETING A ROW

Sometimes you discover that you have too many rows or columns. Deleting a row is as easy as inserting one—and performed in a similar fashion. Using either QuickMenu or the Table pulldown menu:

- Choose Delete. The Delete dialog box will appear.
- Key the number of columns or rows you want to delete, and then choose Delete.

On second thought, you decide that you do not need to have the blank line between the table title and the columns titles.

▶ **EXERCISE 12-10**

1. Place your Insertion Point in the row to be deleted.
2. Choose QuickMenu, and then choose Delete and Rows.
3. Key the number of rows (1), if necessary. Then click on OK.
4. Close the file without saving it.

DELETING A TABLE

You can delete most features in WordPerfect by simply deleting their codes in Reveal Codes. However, you cannot delete the **[Tbl Def:]** code with one keystroke. This helps protect you from losing what may be many long hours of work in defining a table.

When you try to delete a table with Backspace or Delete, the Delete Table dialog box will appear.
(See Figure 12-9.)

Figure 12-9
Delete Table dialog box

On this dialog box, WordPerfect allows you to delete an entire table, just the table contents, or just the structure of a table (leaving the text intact). If you delete the structure of a table without deleting any of the text within that table, a tab will be placed between each cell and a hard return will be placed between each line. The text in each column will be aligned according to current tab settings. Therefore, you might want to move the Insertion Point above the table *before* you delete it, display the Ruler Bar, and set tabs so that they correspond to the columns in the table. By doing this, when you delete the table, the text in the columns will still be aligned and spaced correctly.

1. Open the file named **invoice.rev.**
2. Select the entire table by displaying either the left arrow or up arrow inside the table and triple-clicking on the left mouse button.
3. Press **Backspace** or **Delete.** The Delete Table dialog box will appear.
4. Make the appropriate choice concerning what you want to delete; in this case, Table Structure, and then choose OK.
5. Close this file without saving the changes.

▶ **EXERCISE 12-11**

FLOATING CELLS AND SPREADSHEETS

If you use spreadsheet programs, you probably have noticed the similarity between WordPerfect's tables and a typical spreadsheet layout. Both arrange data in rows and columns, and the intersection of a row and a column is a cell. Tables are very useful to arrange and format information, but now they also can be used to prepare mini-spreadsheets and perform many spreadsheet functions. One of WordPerfect's unique new features, floating cells, provides the capability to use table functions and formulas in the body of your text. For many WordPerfect users, the spreadsheet capabilities within WordPerfect will be enough to perform all the spreadsheet functions they need.

You can learn more about both floating cells and WordPerfect's spreadsheet functions by referring to the Reference Manual or User's Guide.

REVIEW

TRUE/FALSE

Circle the correct answer.

1. T F You can use either the Layout menu or the Ruler Bar to create a table.

2. T F To move the Insertion Point to the previous cell, press Alt+Tab.

3. T F To deselect highlighted cells, click anywhere in the table.

4. T F Only the cells that are to be formatted or edited should be Selected.

5. T F You can choose size and appearance attributes for text in tables either before or after you key it.

6. T F If you format a table column to have a Number Type of Currency, you will not have to key the dollar sign ($).

COMPLETION

Fill in the blanks.

1. After you create a table, the Insertion Point is placed in cell _____.

2. To move the Insertion Point to the next cell of a table, press_____.

3. WordPerfect automatically inserts new rows or columns immediately _____ the row or column where you place the Insertion Point.

4. Changing the width of a column is easier using the Tables Column Format dialog box when you need to attain an _____ measurement.

5. One way to work fast with tables is to use the _____ Button Bar.

6. You can delete a table, table contents, or just the table _____, which will leave the text intact but change the appearance.

Troubleshooting with Reveal Codes: When you expand the Table Definition code, you see the following:

[Tbl Def: Table C; 1.44"; 0.729"; 1.08"; 1.44"; 0.729"; 1.08"]

What does Table C mean? Describe what the figures in the remainder of the code tell you.

REVIEW EXERCISES

The following exercises give you practice in creating a table. Try to insert the proper commands and codes without referring to the lessons. If, however, you are not sure how to perform a function, look it up and study it carefully so that you will know how to do it in the future.

1. Prepare the table and key the text shown in Figure 12-10.
2. Place a double line between the table title and column titles and use a 10% fill in the title rows.
3. Join cells as appropriate for the titles.
4. Use center, currency, left justify, and decimal alignment as appropriate for the columns.
5. Adjust the column widths and margins for a more attractive table.
6. Save this file with the name **disks.** Print one copy and Close the file.

SPECIAL PURCHASE ON DISKS		
Stock No.	Description	Flyer Price
X2383	3 1/2" DD Formatted	$5.89
X4143	3 1/2" HD Formatted (11-Pack)	$6.99
X3525	5 1/4" DD Formatted	$3.89
X6470	5 1/4" HD Formatted	$5.89

Figure 12-10

Prepare a table of ten of your closest friends' names, addresses, and telephone numbers. You may design this table in whatever manner you choose—just make use of column titles and make some variations in type style and size. Save this file with the name **friends.nos.** Print one copy and Close the file.

LESSON 13

Columns

OBJECTIVES

Upon completion of this lesson, you will be able to:
1. Format documents using newspaper columns.
2. Format documents using balanced newspaper columns.
3. Format documents using parallel columns.

You will find the WordPerfect Columns feature helpful for situations in which you have text to put into columns. There are two basic types of columns: Newspaper and Parallel.

Newspaper columns are used for text that flows from the bottom of one column to the top of the next, as in newspapers, newsletters, and brochures. You can have **Balanced Newspaper columns**, which are similar to regular Newspaper columns, but each column is adjusted on the page so they are equal in length.

Parallel columns are used where related sections of text remain next to each other across the page, as in scripts, resumes, and lists. **Parallel columns with Block Protect** keep each row of columns together. If a column in one row becomes so long that it moves across a page break, both columns move to the next page.

Gutter width is the width of the blank spacing between columns.

CREATING NEWSPAPER COLUMNS

When Newspaper columns are used, text wraps from the bottom of one column up to the top of the next column. When all columns on the page are filled, text spills into the first column on the next page. Text continues to flow smoothly from one column to the next, even if text is added or deleted.

DEFINING AND CHANGING NEWSPAPER COLUMN MARGINS

There are two ways to define and change Newspaper column margins: with the Power Bar and with the Columns dialog box. Notice how the two methods differ.

- Click on the Columns button on the Power Bar.

You can choose two, three, four, or five evenly spaced newspaper columns by dragging the mouse pointer down and clicking on your choice. In each case, the gutter width remains fixed at 0.5 inch. If any of these settings are not acceptable, you can click on Define and the Columns dialog box will appear. (See Figure 13-1.)

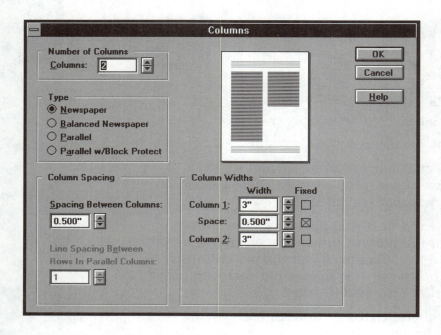

Figure 13-1
Columns dialog box

or

- Choose Layout, Columns, and Define.

The dialog box will appear, showing the default settings and a Preview box which shows how your choices will look on the page as you make them.

Throughout this lesson, you are to perform a series of exercises in which you will learn to create columns. Follow along carefully.

In this exercise, you will learn how to define Newspaper columns through the dialog box:

▶ **EXERCISE 13-1**

1. Choose Layout, Columns, and Define.

2. Key the Number of Columns on the page; in this case, 2. (Through the dialog box, you can create up to 24 side-by-side columns.)

3. Select the Type; in this case, Newspaper. The default 0.5 inch gutter is too wide, so choose Space Between Columns and key 0.25. You can insert either a decimal value or a fraction. Choose OK or press **Enter** when you are satisfied with your settings.

4. Now choose Insert and File (this is a case where you want to bring a file into the one you have already started on screen), and then choose the document named **security.1** after the Insertion Point. Note that it will appear on the screen as a two-page, two-column document. Save this file as **newspap1,** Print one copy, and Close the file.

THE STATUS BAR

The column number of the column in which you are working is indicated in the middle of the Status Bar.

USING THE RULER BAR

You can also set your gutter width and size of columns by displaying the Ruler Bar (Choose View and then Ruler Bar), clicking on the gutter and left and right margin arrows, and moving them where you want them.

 In this exercise, you will use the Power Bar and see columns on the Ruler Bar:

▶ **EXERCISE 13-2**

1. Open the **security.1** file.

2. Move the Insertion Point to the place you want columns to start; in this case, at the beginning of the fifth paragraph starting with `Other related issues....`

3. Click on the Columns button on the Power Bar.

The options shown in Figure 13-2 will appear; note that you can create up to five columns.

Figure 13-2
Columns drop-down menu from Columns button.

LESSON 13 COLUMNS **WP165**

4. Move the selection bar down to highlight the desired number of columns and release the mouse button to select it. For this exercise, select 3 Columns. The text from the Insertion Point on appears in three columns. Note that the Ruler Bar shows the margins for each column.

5. Save this file as **newspap2** and Close the file.

From now on, you can choose either the Dialog Box *or* Power Bar and Ruler Bar method of creating columns. The latter is easier and faster; but if you need more than five columns or want to enter exact measurements, you need to use the Columns dialog box.

The instructions for creating columns can be used either to format a document that has already been created or to create columns for a document that has not yet been keyed. If you Select a block of text that has been created before you define columns, WordPerfect puts the Column Definition code at the beginning of the block and automatically turns columns off at the end of the block.

CHANGING THE NUMBER OF COLUMNS

You can be anywhere in the columns and change the number of the columns. What happens is that WordPerfect locates the previous column definition, updates it, and makes it the new selection. This is a quick and easy way to change, for example, from three to two columns.

PUTTING PART OF A DOCUMENT IN COLUMNS

For variation in the layout and format of a document, you may want only part of a document in columns. You can put part of a document in columns by selecting (highlighting) a section of text, and then going into columns and choosing the number of columns. Just the highlighted section of text will be put in columns.

STARTING A NEW COLUMN

Also, for variation in the layout and format of a document, you may want to end one column and begin another column. Columns are separated by Column Break codes. When keying a document, to start a *new* column:

- Click on the Columns button on the Power Bar and click on Column Break on the drop-down menu, *or*
- Choose Layout, Columns, and then Column Break, *or*
- Press **Ctrl+Enter** to create a column break.

The Column Break command will insert the Hard Column code **[HCol]**, which indicates the beginning of a new column. You can tell which column and page you are in by looking at the status line at the bottom of the screen.

MOVING WITHIN AND BETWEEN NEWSPAPER COLUMNS

To move from column to column:

- Move the mouse pointer to the desired location and click, *or*
- Press **Alt+Right Arrow** to move to the column to the right or press **Alt+Left Arrow** to move to the column to the left.

All other movement keys will function as they usually do, except that they will move the Insertion Point within the margins of the current column instead of within the margins of the page. For example, pressing End moves the Insertion Point to the end of the line in the current column, not to the end of the line in the far right column.

UNDERSTANDING TAB SETTINGS IN COLUMNS

As you may remember, tabs are normally set relative to the left margin. If the left margin changes, the tab settings move with it. Tabs are set relative not only to the left margin of the document, but also to the left margin of *each* column.

TURNING COLUMNS OFF

To turn Columns off:

- Choose Layout, Columns, and Off, *or*
- Choose Columns Off from the Power Bar's drop-down menu.

You can delete columns by dragging the Column Definition code **[Col Def]** out of the Reveal Codes window. If you mistakenly delete a Column Definition code, immediately choose Undo from the Edit menu.

BALANCED NEWSPAPER COLUMNS

With Balanced Newspaper columns, WordPerfect automatically adjusts the length of all columns so that they end at approximately the same line. Any text that follows a Column Off code appears on the same page, but is not in columns format. When you turn off normal Newspaper columns, the cursor automatically moves to the top of the next page.

You create Balanced Newspaper columns by using the Columns dialog box in the same way that you create normal Newspaper columns, except that you choose the Balance Newspaper type instead of Newspaper.

1. Open the **security.1** file.
2. Choose Layout, Columns, and Define and the Columns dialog box will appear.
3. For this exercise, choose 3 columns and Balanced Newspaper.
4. Since a gutter width of 0.50 is rather large, change Spacing between Columns to 0.30.
5. Save this file as **newscol.bal.** Print a copy and Close the file.

You decide that it may look better if you put only part of the document in columns.

1. Open the **security.1** file.
2. Select (highlight) the two paragraphs beginning with A virus is one of....
3. Click on the Columns button on the Power Bar and choose Define.
4. For this exercise, choose 2 columns and Balanced Newspaper.
5. Set a gutter width of 0.35.
6. Save this file as **newscol2.bal.** Print a copy and Close the file.

CREATING PARALLEL COLUMNS

Parallel columns are very useful for documents that require related sections of text to be printed side by side across the page. If text is added or deleted in Parallel columns, the sections still remain parallel to each other. Parallel columns can be used for schedules, agendas, resumes, or scripts, as shown in Figure 13-3.

JULIET	How cam'st thou hither, tell me, and wherefore? The orchard walls are high and hard to climb, And the place death, considering who thou art, If any of my kinsmen find thee here.
ROMEO	With love's light wings did I o'erperch these walls, For stony limits cannot hold love out, And what love can do, that dares love attempt: Therefore thy kinsmen are no stop to me.

JULIET	If they do see thee, they will murder thee.
ROMEO	Alack, there lies more peril in thine eye than twenty of their swords. Look thou but sweet and I am proof against their enmity.
JULIET	I would not for the world they saw thee here.
ROMEO	I have night's cloak to hide me from their eyes, And but thou love me, let them find me here. My life were better ended by their hate. Than death prorogued, wanting of thy love.

Figure 13-3

KEYING TEXT IN PARALLEL COLUMNS

In the following exercise, you will learn to key text in Parallel columns.

EXERCISE 13-5

1. Choose Layout, Columns, and then Define, OR click on the Columns button on the Power Bar and then on Define. You can also double-click on the Columns button on the Power Bar to get the Define Columns dialog box to appear.

2. Choose Parallel and choose OK.

3. To make the left column narrower than the right column, drag to the left the gray space on the Ruler Bar that represents the space between the two columns (also known as the gutter space). Set the Ruler Bar markers for the gutter at 2.5" and 3", as shown in Figure 13-4.

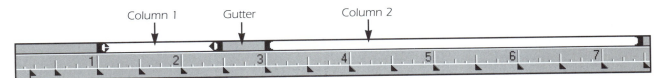

Figure 13-4
Ruler Bar showing columns and gutter

4. Now that the page is prepared, you can start keying the text of the script shown in Figure 13-3 into columns.

5. Key the text to appear in the first column; in this case, JULIET. Then create a hard column break (press **Ctrl+Enter**).

6. Key the text of Juliet's dialog and place a hard column break at the end.

7. Continue to key text and to place a hard column break at the end of each section. When you place a hard column break in the last column of the line, the column is turned off and a new column line is turned on.

8. When you are finished keying, save the file with the name **script.** Print a copy and Close the file.

In those situations where you want to protect blocks of text from being split by a page break, choose Parallel with Block Protect when you define columns.

MOVING WITHIN AND BETWEEN PARALLEL COLUMNS

To move to the column to the right or left, press **Alt+Right Arrow** or **Alt+Left Arrow**, or position the mouse pointer and click.

Pressing the **Up Arrow** and **Down Arrow** keys moves the Insertion Point up and down, line by line, within the same column.

If you want to move up or down quickly through the sections of either newspaper or parallel text, regardless of the number of lines in each section, you can press **Ctrl+Up Arrow** and **Ctrl+Down Arrow**. These keystrokes move the Insertion Point to the first character in each section of parallel text.

REVIEW

TRUE/FALSE

Circle the correct answer.

1. T F   When desired, you can use a combination of text in columns and text flowing across the page.
2. T F   The Column Break command will insert the Hard Column code **[HCol]** to indicate the beginning of a new column.
3. T F   You can set the distance between columns and the width of columns on the Ruler Bar.
4. T F   Parallel columns are very useful for documents that require related sections of text to be printed side by side.
5. T F   To move to either the Newspaper or Parallel column to the right or left, press Alt+Right Arrow or Alt+Left Arrow.
6. T F   You can use either the Columns dialog box or the Power Bar to create columns.

COMPLETION

Fill in the blanks.

1. The two basic types of columns are _____ and _____.
2. With _____ _____ columns, WordPerfect automatically adjusts the length of all columns so that they end at approximately the same line.
3. _____ columns are used for text that flows from the bottom of one column to the top of the next.
4. To create a script, you should use _____ columns.
5. _____ width is the width of the blank spacing between columns.

Troubleshooting with Reveal Codes: When you print the newsletter you prepared, the columns are of uneven length. When you click on the **[Col Def]** code in Reveal Codes, you see the following:

[Col Def:Newspaper, Total:2,Col[Adj],Gut[0.5"],Col[Adj]]

Explain what the code is telling you? Why are the columns of uneven length?

REVIEW EXERCISE

Create the resume shown in Figure 13-5. After keying the telephone number, define two Parallel columns. Set the left column with margins of 1" and 2.5" and the right columns with margins of 3" and 7.5". Leave .5" between columns. You may use whatever typeface you desire. To follow good design principles, however, you should use the same typeface throughout the entire document, but with a variety of type sizes such as 24 pt., 18 pt., and 12 pt. Save the document with the name **resume1**. Print a copy and Close the file.

REVIEW EXERCISE 13-1

George R. Ward

803 East Burlington   Davenport, Iowa   52803   319–555–6864

Objective — To use the skills I have learned thus far in my career to help a company succeed in its purposes.

Education — Graduated Central High School
Hendersonville, TN   1986

Memphis State University
Took evening courses 1987–1991

Experience — 1991–present
St. Lukes Memorial Hospital, Davenport, IA
Volunteer

1991–present
Larry Dean Construction, Davenport, IA
Payroll Supervisor

1989–1991
Larry Dean Construction, Memphis, TN
Payroll and Accounts Receivable Clerk

1987–1989
Wal–Mart, Memphis, TN
Clerk

1986–1987
Chicken Shack, Chattanooga, TN
Cook and Waiter

Interests — Swimming, hiking, reading

References — References available upon request.

■ Figure 13-5

LESSON 14

Merge

OBJECTIVES

Upon completion of this lesson, you will be able to:

1. Create a data file.
2. Create a form file.
3. Print letters and envelopes using merge.
4. Perform a merge of a data file and form file.
5. Perform a keyboard merge.

Merge is the process of combining information from two or more sources into a single new document. Merge is most useful for repetitive activity. For example, one of the most common uses of merge is to combine a form letter with a list of names and addresses so that personalized letters can be prepared automatically. You can also use merge to create contracts, phone lists, and a variety of other documents in which you bring information from two or more files together into one.

The three basic steps involved in using WordPerfect's Merge feature are:

1. Create the **data file**, such as a list of names and addresses.
2. Create the **form file**, such as a form letter.
3. Perform the merge; that is, merge the two files to create a third **merged document file** to be printed.

In addition, with WordPerfect 6.0 for Windows you can merge names and addresses to print envelopes to accompany letters.

The most common type of merge combines a data file with a form file. The document that supplies the data for the form file is usually a WordPerfect data file, although you can also use information from a database file such as dBase or Paradox, from a spreadsheet file, or from the keyboard.

CREATING A DATA FILE

The data file contains variable data; that is, the information which changes from document to document. The smallest unit of data is called a **field**. The number of fields will vary, depending upon the number of variables you might want. In this lesson, six fields—the recipient's first name, last name, street address, city, state, and ZIP code—make up the basic information in a mailing list. These fields will be merged with each form letter.

A **record** contains a group of related fields. For example, all the information related to a single person or company makes up a record, and a similar record will be created for each person on the mailing list. A different project might call for a different set of variables, but the information will still need to be placed into fields and records.

The data file contains the information that is to be inserted into the form file. For example, if you are sending out form letters, the data file will contain the list of names and addresses. The data file usually contains a list of names and addresses, but it can contain any type of information which you might merge into a form file. For example, it can contain data about all the companies you do business with, including their contact person, the amount of sales you do with them, etc.

Throughout this lesson, you are to perform a series of exercises in which you will learn to create a data file, a form file, and to merge files and print envelopes. Follow along carefully.

The following steps explain how to create a data file containing five records. You will merge the information in this file with the form letter file which you will create.

▶ **EXERCISE 14-1**

1. Choose <u>T</u>ools and then <u>M</u>erge. The Merge dialog box shown in Figure 14-1 will appear.

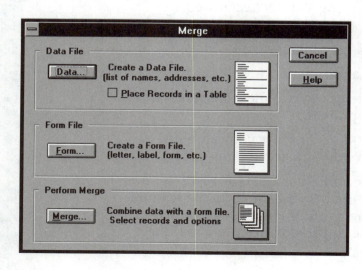

Figure 14-1
Merge dialog box

WP176   LESSON 14   MERGE

2. To create a data text file, click on Data.

If you already have a document in the active window, you are prompted to choose a new window or use the file in the active window.

3. In this case, click on New Document Window, if necessary, and then on OK. The Create Data File dialog box shown in Figure 14-2 will appear. At the same time, the Merge Feature Bar will appear on the screen. To name fields, key the name of a field, and then choose Add (or press **Enter**). Using many fields gives you more flexibility. For example, having a ZIP code field separate from the address field lets you create a POSTNET bar code to be printed on an envelope.

Figure 14-2
Create Data File dialog box

4. In this exercise, key first name for the first field and click on Add or press **Enter.** You will see "first name" in the Field Name List.

5. Key last name and click on Add.

6. Key address and click on Add.

7. Key city and click on Add.

8. Key state and click on Add.

9. Key ZIP and click on Add. Click on OK to indicate that you have completed specifying the number of fields you want. The Quick Data Entry dialog box shown in Figure 14-3 will appear.

In the Quick Data Entry dialog box, you should key the information for each field in the record, and then click on Next Field. You can also move to the next field by pressing **Enter**. To add a line to a field, such as an address, press **Ctrl+Enter.** The number of lines in a field can vary from record to record. For example, an address field in one record may be two lines, while in another it may be three lines, and in another, only one line.

To edit field names as you are naming them, you should highlight and click on the field name in the Field Names List box. The field name will appear in the Field Name text box, where you can correct it. Choose Replace to put the corrected version in the list. If you decide you don't want one of the field names, highlight and click on it in the Field Names List box, and then choose Delete.

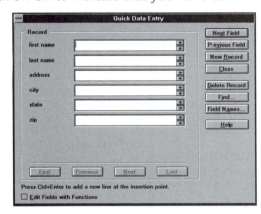

Figure 14-3
Quick Data Entry dialog box

The type of information in a given field should be the same from record to record. For example, the city field in each record should contain only the city. Once in a while, although not in this exercise, you will come to a field where you don't have anything to key for a certain person. When this happens, just press **Enter** to skip that field, leaving it blank.

10. Key the following information in the appropriate fields now:

```
Amy
Behrens
2300 East Eighth Street
Muncie
IN
47306
```

When you have keyed all the fields in a record, choose New Record. To delete a record, choose First, Previous, Next, or Last to display the records, and then choose Delete Record.

To change field names, choose Field Names, make your editing changes, and then choose OK.

11. Continue keying the information for the next four records shown in Figure 14-4. If an error is noted in a previous field, press Pre*v*ious Field to move the Insertion Point back. Then choose Close.

```
Christina
Hammitt
1503 National Road
Hartford
CT
06102

Wayne
Coil
RR 2, Box 135
Dunkirk
IN
47336

Byung-Woo
Park
3501 Godman Avenue
Chicago
IL
60617

Maria
Garcia
405 South Morrison
Tucson
AZ
85726
```

Figure 14-4

12. To save the data file, choose Yes, Save the file as **names.dat**, and then choose OK.

You should use the same extension, such as **.dat**, for all the data files you create. This will remind you that the file is a data file.

Your final results should look like Figure 14-5. Note that WordPerfect has automatically inserted an ENDFIELD code at the end of each field and an ENDRECORD code at the end of each record.

```
FIELDNAMES(first name;last name;
address;city;state;ZIP) ENDRECORD

AmyENDFIELD
BehrensENDFIELD
2300 East Eighth StreetENDFIELD
MuncieENDFIELD
INENDFIELD
47306ENDFIELD
ENDRECORD

ChristinaENDFIELD
HammittENDFIELD
412 South Main StreetENDFIELD
HartfordENDFIELD
CTENDFIELD
06102ENDFIELD
ENDRECORD

WayneENDFIELD
CoilENDFIELD
RR 2, Box 135ENDFIELD
DunkirkENDFIELD
INENDFIELD
47336ENDFIELD
ENDRECORD

Byung-WooENDFIELD
ParkENDFIELD
3501 Godman AvenueENDFIELD
ChicagoENDFIELD
ILENDFIELD
60617ENDFIELD
ENDRECORD
```

```
MariaENDFIELD
GarciaENDFIELD
405 South MorrisonENDFIELD
TucsonENDFIELD
AZENDFIELD
85726ENDFIELD
ENDRECORD
```

Figure 14-5

PRINT DATA TEXT FILES

To print data text files:

1. Choose Options on the Merge Feature Bar shown in Figure 14-6.

2. Then choose Print.
3. Click on OK to print with no page breaks between records and without the codes. Warning: If you do not print the data file through Options, each of the records will be printed on a separate page.
4. Close the file.

Figure 14-6
Merge Feature bar

▶ EXERCISE 14-2

CREATING A FORM FILE

You must create a form file before you can use Merge. The form file acts as a form or template. It contains the information that remains the same for every merged document. For example, if you are sending a form letter to several people, the body of the letter would be the form file and it would be the same for each person. A form file also contains merge codes that retrieve specific information from data files.

The merge codes are really programming commands that you insert in a form file. They can be as simple as a FIELD or DATE code. When you insert a FIELD code, the corresponding field in the data file will be inserted during the merge.

To create a form file, perform the following steps exactly as directed:

1. Choose Tools and then Merge. The Merge dialog box will appear. Choose Form.
2. Click on New Document Window and then on OK.

When you use Merge, you can **associate** a form file with a data file. This means that whenever you open a form file, you can merge it with the associated data file without having to specify a path and file name.

▶ EXERCISE 14-3

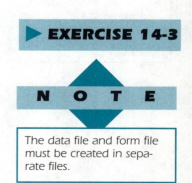

N O T E

The data file and form file must be created in separate files.

WP180   LESSON 14   MERGE

3. To associate this file with a data file, click on Data File, specify **names.dat,** and then choose OK.

4. Key the form letter exactly as it looks in Figure 14-7. Use Left justification for the body of the letter, with the date ending flush with the right margin. The complimentary close and signature lines should begin at the center. Center the letter vertically on the page. Save this letter with the name **merge.let.**

```
                                           November 15, 199-
(Leave 3 blank lines here)
Dear

On behalf of the men, women, and children whose
Thanksgiving season will be made a little brighter,
thank you for your recent gift to the Middletown
Mission.

Your generosity--and that of many others--will enable
us to serve a hot, nutritious meal to many hungry and
lonely individuals who will join us for a time of
thanksgiving and fellowship.  Your support will help
us care for those who  have nowhere else to turn not
only during the holiday, but also throughout the year.

All of us here at the Middletown Mission are truly
grateful for people like you--friends who practice
caring, loving, and giving every day of the year and
give sacrificially so that others might have a better
life.

Thank you again for your gift.  You and your family
will be in our thoughts this holiday season and
year around.

                         Sincerely,

                         (Insert 3 blank lines here)

                         Ray S. Reece
                         Executive Director
```

■ Figure 14-7

To set up the form file, you will use this letter and insert the codes to direct WordPerfect to merge in the information from the data file. Wherever information is needed from the data file, a {Field} merge code is placed in the data file. The {Field} code includes the name of the field which should be inserted into the letter.

The position of the {Field} code and field name tells WordPerfect where the information from the field should be inserted into the letter. For example {Field}**first name** tells WordPerfect to insert the first name wherever it encounters this code. During a merge, only those fields that have been specified by the form file will be merged.

In this exercise, the first field in each record contains the person's first name. The second field contains the person's last name; the third contains the person's address; the fourth contains the city; the fifth contains the state; and the sixth contains the ZIP code. In this exercise, you will use the first field with the person's first name in the salutation.

To put the fields in the proper position, work carefully through the following steps:

▶ **EXERCISE 14-4**

1. With **merge.let** on the screen, place the Insertion Point at the left margin, at the beginning of the line above the salutation. You want to insert the codes as shown in Figure 14-8.

Do **NOT** key FIELD or the name of the field. You MUST choose the appropriate WordPerfect commands to enter these codes.

```
                                            November 15, 199-

FIELD(first name) FIELD(last name)
FIELD(address)
FIELD(city), FIELD(state) FIELD(ZIP)
Dear FIELD(first name):
On behalf of the men, women, and children whose
Thanksgiving season will be made a little brighter,
thank you for your recent gift to the Middletown
Mission.
```

▌ Figure 14-8

2. Click on the Insert Field button on the Merge Feature Bar. With **first name** highlighted, click on Insert. Press the **Space Bar** once.

3. Highlight **last name** and click on Insert. Press **Enter** once.

4. Continue with this process, noting carefully where to place spaces and hard returns to properly place the remainder of the FIELD codes for the inside address and the first name in the salutation. Remember to key a comma after the city code and a colon after the salutation.

5. When you have completed entering the FIELD code commands, click on Close.

6. Save this file as **mergelet.for.**

Using the extension **.for** will remind you that this is a form file.

7. Close the file.

PRINTING LETTERS AND ENVELOPES USING MERGE

In all probability, you will want an envelope for each of your merged letters. WordPerfect makes this easy. You will learn how by performing each of the steps in the following exercise.

EXERCISE 14-5

1. Start with a blank document screen.
2. Select Tools and then Merge. The Merge dialog box will appear. Click on Merge.

The Perform Merge dialog box shown in Figure 14-9 will appear.

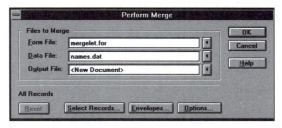

Figure 14-9
Perform Merge dialog box to be used with envelopes

3. In the form file, you should have **mergelet.for** as the name of the desired form file. Press **Tab** to move to the Data File text box, which should already have **names.dat** because it is the associated file. Enter these file names if they are not already there.
4. Then choose the Envelopes button at the bottom of the dialog box; if the Insertion Point is not in the Return Address text box, click in the Return Address text box and key your own return address. If you are using preprinted envelopes, you should not key your return address. Then move the Insertion Point to the Mailing Address text box.
5. Choose the Field button at the bottom of the dialog box to see a list of your available fields. Double-click on the first field you want on the envelope; in this case, the first name field. Press the **Space Bar.**
6. Again click on the Field button to bring up the Insert Field Name or Number dialog box. Double-click on the last name field. Then press **Enter.**
7. Continue this process until you have all the field names the merge will need for the address. Be sure to enter spaces, punctuation, and returns in the proper places.
8. Once everything is set in this dialog box, choose OK to go back to the Perform Merge dialog box and then choose OK to start the merge.

As WordPerfect merges the form and data files, a screen message will show as each record is merged. If you need to stop a merge in process, press Cancel on this message box. You should not save the merged document because it takes up disk space and can be easily merged again.

When the merge is finished, your letters are at the top of the document file and the corresponding envelopes are at the bottom. You should scroll through your merged file to see if you have achieved what you intended. If any merged document does not come out properly, check the fields in your form document to make sure that they have been set up properly. When you print this document, all letters will be printed first and the printer will pause for you to load the envelopes to be printed; unless you have a special feeder for the envelopes, in which case the envelopes will be printed automatically immediately after the letters.

Because there is a great variety of printer types on the market, there can be some differences in how they print. If you have trouble printing envelopes, see your instructor for help with printing envelopes on your printer.

9. Check with your instructor to determine where you should print this file.
10. Close the file without saving it.

PERFORMING THE MERGE WITHOUT ENVELOPES

You will not want to address envelopes for all types of merged documents. Work carefully through the following exercise to learn how to merge only the letters.

1. Start with a blank document screen.
2. Select Tools and then Merge. The Merge dialog box will appear. Click on Merge.

The Perform Merge dialog box shown in Figure 14-10 will appear.

EXERCISE 14-6

Figure 14-10
Perform Merge dialog box to be used without envelopes

3. Key **mergelet.for** as the name of the desired form file in the Form File text box and click OK.

When you have already chosen the associated file, WordPerfect will perform the merge immediately. When the merge is completed, the Insertion Point is at the bottom of the last merged document.

You should *not* save the merged document because it takes up disk space and can be easily merged again.

Although you have prepared only five letters in this exercise, you would use the same procedure to prepare a form letter to be sent to many people on a mailing list—even hundreds and thousands!

PERFORMING A KEYBOARD MERGE

You may find yourself in the situation where you send a certain form letter often, but to only one person at a time. Keyboard merge is the best way to do this because a Keyboard command prompts you to key the information needed.

You can perform a keyboard merge easily by preparing a form letter specifically for this purpose or by modifying a form letter you already have prepared.

In the following exercise, we will perform a keyboard merge, so follow along carefully.

▶ **EXERCISE 14-7**

   1. Beginning with a clear screen, open **merge.let.**

2. Choose Merge on the Feature Bar. The Merge dialog box will appear. Choose Form, and then select Use File in Active Window and click on OK.

3. Delete the date given, and click on Date on the Merge Feature Bar.

4. Place the Insertion Point at the left margin on the line above the salutation, where you will want to insert the inside address.

5. Click on Keyboard on the Merge Feature Bar. The Insert Merge Code

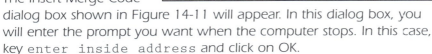

Figure 14-11
Insert Merge Code dialog box

dialog box shown in Figure 14-11 will appear. In this dialog box, you will enter the prompt you want when the computer stops. In this case, key enter inside address and click on OK.

6. Press **Enter** and move the Insertion Point to where you will insert the name in the salutation. Click on Keyboard on the Merge Feature Bar and the Insert Merge Code dialog box will again appear. This time key enter first name: and click on OK. This completes preparation of the letter for the keyboard merge, so Save this letter as **mergelet.key.**

7. To perform the keyboard merge, click on Merge on the Merge Feature Bar, and then click on Merge again. The dialog box should indicate that the current document will be merged and there are no associated files. If the data file does not say None, click on the arrow at the end of the box and select None. Click on OK.

The keyboard merge document will appear on the screen with the Insertion Point at the first place for you to insert. The Merge Message prompt shown in Figure 14-12 will appear.

Figure 14-12
Merge Message prompt

8. You should enter the following inside address:

```
Tara Richardson
2300 Grand Avenue
Francesville, IN  47946
```

Press **Alt+Enter,** OR click on Continue. If you click on Quit, WordPerfect will go to the end of the document and ignore all merge codes. If you click on Stop, the merge will stop at this point.

9. Another Message prompt will appear. This time you should enter the first name and the colon, Tara:. Press **Alt+Enter.** The merging will take place immediately.

10. Print one copy of this letter. You could print an envelope for this letter by clicking on the Envelope icon on the Button Bar at this time. You need not do so in this lesson.

11. Save the file as **tara.let,** Close the file, and Close the keyboard merge file.

As you can see, Merge is a wonderful feature that can save you hours of rekeying if you have a number of letters and envelopes to create. Keyboard merge is also a great timesaver if you send the same form letter often, but to only one or two persons at a time.

REVIEW

TRUE/FALSE

Circle the correct answer.

1. T F One of the most common uses of Merge is to create personalized form letters.
2. T F The number of fields in a data file will differ according to the number of variables.
3. T F The position of the {**Field**} code indicates the place where the information from the field should be inserted.
4. T F The form file contains the information to be inserted into the data file.
5. T F A form merge is a great timesaver if you send the same form letter often, but to only one or two persons at a time.
6. T F You can perform a merge of letters either with or without envelopes.

COMPLETION

Fill in the blanks.

1. A _____ _____ contains merge codes that retrieve specific information from data files.
2. If you will always use a certain data file with a certain form file, you should _____ the files.
3. _____ _____ codes are used to divide fields and _____ _____ codes are used to divide records.
4. You should not save the merged document because it takes up _____ _____ and can be easily merged again.
5. A _____ command pauses a merge and prompts you to key the information needed.
6. A _____ contains a group of related fields.

Troubleshooting with Reveal Codes: Look at the codes and determine why the address is not printing correctly. Explain your answer.

FIELD(first name) FIELD(last name)

FIELD(address)

FIELD(city)FIELD(state)FIELD(ZIP)

REVIEW EXERCISES

REVIEW EXERCISE 14-1

Create the memorandum shown in Figure 14-13 as a form file document to be distributed internally to some of your employees. Their names are to be merged into the document, and the Date Code should be used so that the date will remain current. In addition, each employee's ZIP code should be merged into the document where indicated. Center the title Memorandum in uppercase and bold at the top of the document. Prepare the memorandum as a fully justified document.

You will use the data file **names.dat** which you prepared in Exercise 14-1, so plan this document to use the appropriate field names from that data file. Save this document with the name **zipmemo.for.**

```
                        MEMORANDUM
TO:     {First Name} {Last Name}
FROM:   HUMAN RESOURCES DEPARTMENT
DATE:   Date Code
SUBJECT:   FULL ZIP CODES

It has recently come to our attention that our
records are incomplete concerning each of your ZIP
code extensions. Our records indicate that your ZIP
code is {ZIP code}.

Please call this department at 555-4782 to provide
us with your correct ZIP code extension.

Thank you for your cooperation in this matter.
```

Figure 14-13

REVIEW EXERCISE 14-2

Perform the merge of the **zipmemo.for** and **names.dat** files. Print the merged file.

LESSON 15

Labels and Sort

OBJECTIVES

Upon completion of this lesson, you will be able to:

1. Create a label definition.
2. Create and print individual labels.
3. Create and print labels for mass mailings using merge.
4. Sort by ZIP code and last name.

Another great feature of WordPerfect 6.0 for Windows is the ability to create various labels, such as mailing labels, file folder labels, and diskette and videotape labels. Whether you are addressing a single label or printing hundreds of mailing labels, the WordPerfect Labels feature can make the job easier for you.

Whenever you want to print on paper that is not the standard 8.5" x 11" size, you must select the appropriate size and type. If the size and type of label you want has not been created, you can create it. The definition you create can be used once and then deleted, or it can be saved for repeated use.

LABEL DEFINITIONS

To place text correctly on the labels, WordPerfect uses a series of measurements, including the size and number of labels, the placement of labels on the sheet, the distance between labels, and the margin settings for individual labels. The Labels feature lets you select a predefined label definition or define the exact size yourself.

SELECTING A LABEL DEFINITION

Throughout this lesson, you are to perform a series of exercises in which you will learn to create and work with labels. Follow along carefully.

1. Begin with a blank document window.
2. Choose Layout and then Labels to bring up the Labels dialog box shown in Figure 15-1.

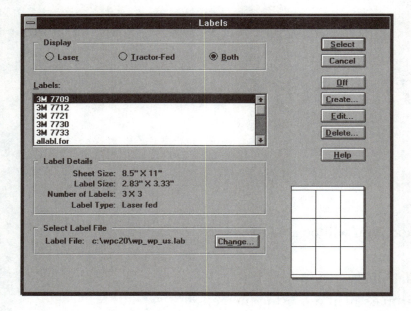

Figure 15-1
Labels dialog box

You must have a laser printer available to complete this lesson exactly as directed. See your instructor for how to adapt these directions to fit your printer.

3. At the top of the dialog box, you are prompted to choose the type of label you will be using. WordPerfect will then display a list of predefined label definitions. For this exercise, click on Both. Notice the list of predefined label definitions. Scroll through the list and stop and look at the characteristics of a definition. Whenever possible, of course, it will be easier for you to use a predefined label definition, either from those provided or one that you create and save for future use.

Notice that there are predefined definitions for name badges, shipping and file folder labels, and index cards and postcards, as well as mailing labels. Notice also, the sizes indicated in the Label Details section and that the type of printer the label works with is indicated. A preview of how the labels are placed on the page is in the lower right-hand corner. Always check to see that this preview is divided in the same way your labels are divided.

The first label in the dialog box is for an arrangement of labels on an 8.5" x 11" sheet. This default is for three labels across and three labels down. There will be a small space above and below the labels on the 11" page.

WordPerfect considers the entire sheet of labels a **physical page**. Each individual label is a **logical page**. The page indicator (Pg) on the Status Bar shows which logical page (label) you are on.

If you want to see the labels as they will be arranged when you print them, you must use Page view. Remember, you can use the Page Zoom Full icon. In Draft view, labels are displayed one above the other on your screen and are separated by a line to indicate a logical page break.

Once you select a label definition, you will enter the text for your labels. You can either key the content of individual labels, or you can create labels for mass mailings by using the Merge and Labels features together.

KEYING TEXT IN LABELS

When keying labels, you should use the following keystrokes:

Press	To
Ctrl+Enter (Hard Page)	End the current label and move to the next label
Enter	End a line of text within a label
Alt+PgDn or **Alt+PgUp**	Move to the next or previous label
Ctrl+G, then specify a page	Move to a specific label

For address labels, we will work with the common arrangement of three labels across and ten labels down.

EXERCISE 15-2

1. From the predefined label list, highlight the Avery 5160. Check the preview to be sure that this is an arrangement of three across and ten down and click on Select. Only the first label displays; the rest of the screen is shaded.

2. Key three labels with the first three names and addresses in the left column of those shown in Figure 15-2. You will be placing the addresses in alphabetical order across the page.

3. Print these labels in the proper format just by clicking on the Print icon. For this exercise, print on a sheet of paper rather than on a sheet of labels.

4. Save this file as **3labls.** Close the file.

```
SHEILA ANDERSON            CHRISTINA HAMMITT         DECEIL MOORE
3403 A LANE APT. 2A        1503 NATIONAL ROAD        2205 PUEBLO DRIVE
LANCASTER PA   17604       HARTFORD CT 06102         OREM UT   84057

AMY BEHRENS                TONY HARTE                BYUNG-WOO PARK
2300 E 8TH STREET          8467 MAPLE TREE DRIVE     3501 GODMAN AVENUE
MUNCIE IN   47306          ELKHART IN   46517        CHICAGO IL 60617

OSAMI BERRY                KATHY HOLSCHER            DONNA PFIESTER110
17 SUNBLEST COURT          7223 BELMONT STREET       EDGEMONT ROADHARRISON
SEATTLE WA   98109         HUNTINGTON WV 25701       IN   47060

SCOTT BLACKBURN            KIM KELLAR                JUAN PHILLIPS
6008 PRIMROSE              1409 W. JACKSON           1195 JOHNSON FORK
KANSAS CITY MO 64108       SAN ANGELO TX   76904     MONTCLAIR NJ   07043

KEVIN BUCKLEY              ROBIN KING                RACHAEL POMEROY
4112 S. MAIN STREET        807 WARWICK DRIVE #2      5521 STATE STREET
SAUSALITO CA   94965       HAMMOND IN   46323        CHICAGO IL 60617

WAYNE COIL                 KAREN KOELSCH             PAUL RENNER
RR 2 BOX 135               4110 S. COWAN ROAD        7132 WOODMAR AVE
DUNKIRK IN   47336         OELWEIN IA   50662        INDIANAPOLIS IN   46251

ELIZABETH DANNER           MICHELLE KRALL            TARA RICHARDSON
301 AIRPARK DRIVE          639 WASHINGTON AVE        2300 GRAND AVENUE
ANNAPOLIS MD   21401       MISHAWAKA IN   46544      FRANCESVILLE IN   47946

MARIA GARCIA               CHI-MING LO               DANIEL SNYDER
405 S. MORRISON            1810 PARKVIEW DRIVE       123 SUNSHINE DRIVE
TUCSON AZ 85726            CINCINNATI OH   45234     SELLERSBURG IN   47272

NAIM GUPTA                 LISA MALCHOW              PAMELA WILSON
718 GEORGIAN DRIVE         4305 W. UNIVERSITY        70 N. LAZY PLACE
INDIANPOLIS IN   46220     ORLANDO FL   32820        ALBUQUERQUE NM   87101

JANNA HALL                 WILLIAM MILLER            MARY ETTA YOHO
9267 W MAIN STREET         807 WARWICK DRIVE #1      608 SHELLBARK
AUSTIN TX 78710            HAMMOND IN 46323          MUNCIE IN   47304
```

Figure 15-2

CREATING LABELS FOR MASS MAILINGS

When you want to create labels for mass mailings or for other projects that involve creating and printing many labels, you need to create a merge data file that includes all the mailing addresses. Then you create a merge form file that contains a label definition and the fields you want on the labels.

EXERCISE 15-3

1. Key all of the names and mailing addresses shown in Figure 15-2 in ALPHABETICAL order as a data file to be merged with the labels form file. Choose Tools, Merge, and Data. Click on New Document window and OK. Use the following fields: first name, last name, address, city, state, and ZIP code.

2. Save this file as **customer.dat** and Close the file.

EXERCISE 15-4

In this exercise, you will create a form file with a label definition. Then you will merge the form file with a data file of names and addresses that you wish to print on labels.

1. Open a new document by choosing File and then New, OR by clicking on the New icon.

2. Choose Layout and then Labels. The Labels dialog box will appear.

3. Select the labels definition to use from the Labels list box; in this case, the Avery 5160 labels. Then choose Select or press **Enter.**

4. Choose Tools and then Merge to open the Merge dialog box; then choose the Form button.

5. If the Create Merge File dialog box appears, choose OK or press **Enter** to use the label form in the active document window.

6. In the Associate a Data File text box, key the name of the data file (in this case, **customer.dat**) to be used when generating the labels during the merge and click on OK.

7. Create the mailing address by inserting the FIELD codes. Choose the Insert Field button on the Merge Feature Bar. When the Insert Field Name or Number dialog box appears, select the field you want to insert in the Field Names list box and choose Insert or press **Enter.** Use the fields: first name, last name, address, city, state, and ZIP code. Don't forget to insert the correct spacing and returns.

8. Choose the Close button.

9. Save the label form as **labels.for.**

10. Because we want each address centered on each label, choose Layout, Page, and Center, and then click on Current and Subsequent Pages and OK.

11. Now you can merge the form file **labels.for** with the data file **customer.dat** to create a label for each record in the customer file. Choose Merge from the Merge Feature Bar and choose Merge again on the next screen.

12. Choose OK to start the merge. When the merge is complete, an address for each label is ready to be printed.

13. Click on the Page Zoom Full icon on the Power Bar. Notice how the logical pages are arranged on the physical page. WordPerfect places the individual labels on the sheet of labels from left to right.

14. Print the labels. For this exercise, you can print on a sheet of paper rather than on a sheet of labels. Then Close the document without Saving it and Close the form file.

Now that you have a data file of customers' names and addresses, you can print labels easily. But remember, you can use the same data file in a merge to print letters and envelopes, too!

SORTING

The Sort function provided by WordPerfect allows you to sort alphabetically or numerically. Records are the items that are sorted in a data file. However, for greater flexibility, records can be sorted in smaller parts. For example, you can sort on fields for such items as ZIP code and last name. By performing the steps in the following exercise, you will learn to do such sorting.

▶ **EXERCISE 15-5**

1. Begin with a blank screen, and open the **customer.dat** file.
2. Choose Tools and then Sort. The Sort dialog box shown in Figure 15-3 will appear.
3. Since you are going to sort a merge data file, be sure to click on Merge Record in the Sort By list.

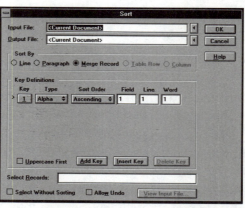

Figure 15-3
Sort dialog box

Use sort **keys** to specify which piece of the record to sort by. Key 1 is the first priority sort, Key 2 is the second, and so on. You can define keys as **alphanumeric** (sorted by letters and digits), **numeric** (sorted by numerical values only), **ascending** (sorted from A to Z and from negative to positive), or **descending** (sorted by letters and numbers in reverse order). Sort keys are not saved when you exit WordPerfect.

4. Since we first want to sort for ZIP code and ZIP code is numeric, change Type to Numeric. Use Ascending sort order. Go to the Field box in Key No. 1, and change the number to 6, since ZIP code is the sixth field in the merge data file.
5. Since we also want to sort on Last Name, we must add another key. Therefore, click on Add Key. Be sure the Type is Alphabetic and use Ascending order. Go to the Field box in Key No. 2, and change the number to 2, since last name is the second field in the merge data file. Click on OK. Look at the file and you will see that it has already been sorted in ZIP code order. In those instances where the ZIP code is the same, the file has been sorted by last name.
6. Print a copy.
7. Save the file as **custsort.dat** and then Close the file.

As you can see, sorting gives you the capability of working with the same files in various ways. For more about sorting in many more ways, see the Reference Manual or User's Guide.

REVIEW

TRUE/FALSE

Circle the correct answer.

1. T F WordPerfect provides you with predefined labels for laser printers only.

2. T F If you want to see the labels as they will be arranged when you print them, you must use Page view.

3. T F WordPerfect places labels on the physical page rom left to right.

4. T F When you are going to do a mass mailing, you should set up your label definition as a part of the data file.

5. T F You can sort text alphabetically or numerically.

6. T F To center each label vertically, you would use the Center Page command.

COMPLETION

Fill in the blanks.

1. If a _____ for the size and type of paper you want has not been created, you can create it.

2. The Labels feature lets you select a predefined label definition or _____ the exact size yourself.

3. The page indicator on the Status Bar shows which _____ _____ you are on.

4. To create labels for mass mailings, you need to create a merge form file that contains a _____ _____ and the _____ you want on the labels.

5. _____ are the items that are sorted in a data file.

6. Use _____ _____ to specify which part of the record to sort by.

Reference Question: Sorting by field is only one method of subdividing records for a Sort. See your Reference Manual or User's Guide and list the four other types of Record Divisions.

LESSON 16

Graphics Borders, Lines, and Boxes

OBJECTIVES

Upon completion of this lesson, you will be able to:

1. Create paragraph, page, and column borders.
2. Create horizontal and vertical graphics lines.
3. Customize or edit horizontal and vertical graphics lines.
4. Create graphics boxes.
5. Vary the appearance of graphics boxes.

In this lesson, you will learn about some of the special graphics features of WordPerfect that can be used to enhance the appearance of your documents.

Throughout the next two lessons, you are to perform a series of exercises in which you will learn to create and work with various graphics capabilities. Follow along carefully.

GRAPHICS BORDERS

You will find the borders capability of WordPerfect useful for enhancing the appearance of paragraphs, columns, or pages. You can use a Paragraph border to attract attention to one particular paragraph of text in a letter or report, for example, or you can add a Page border to each page of a report to guide the reader.

A **fill** attracts attention to the paragraph or page. You can use a fill with a border to emphasize text even more. The fill will not extend beyond the margins. You can also create a fill without using a border.

PARAGRAPH BORDERS

You can create Paragraph borders in two different ways:

Method 1.   Position the Insertion Point at the beginning of the paragraph where you want the border to begin and create the border. Then all of the following text will be within a Paragraph border, *or*

Method 2.   Select (highlight) specific text and then create the border. Only the Selected text will be within the border.

Let's try Method 1.

1. With a blank screen, choose Layout, Paragraph, and Border/Fill. The Paragraph Border dialog box shown in Figure 16-1 will appear.

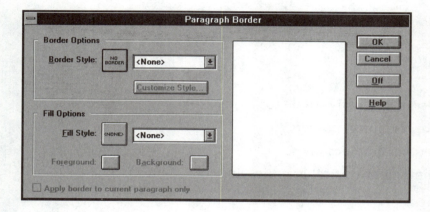

Figure 16-1
Paragraph Border dialog box

2. In the Border Style area, click on the box which says No Border and you will see the examples of the various borders available to you. If you click on the arrow instead, you will see a list of the same borders.

3. Select a border style by clicking on it; in this case, the first one illustrated in the third row (Double).

4. In the same dialog box, you can choose a shade, pattern, or fill style from the Fill Style box or by clicking the arrow. In this case, select the second one illustrated in the first row (10% Fill).

5. Click on Apply border to current paragraph only. (If Apply border to current paragraph only is not selected, the border will surround the current paragraph and all subsequent paragraphs in the document.) Click on OK.

6. Key the text shown in Figure 16-2 on the next page.

7. Your final document should look like Figure 16-2. Save this file as **border. par**, Print a copy, and Close the file.

```
You can use a variety of line styles and thicknesses
with Page and Paragraph borders.  A Paragraph border
is a frame or box that surrounds the text in a given
paragraph.  WordPerfect defines a paragraph as any
amount of text followed by a hard return.  Therefore,
you can have only one character or word followed by a
hard return and surround it with a border.  However,
you should know that the Paragraph border will extend
from the left margin to the right margin.  So if you
want the box to be smaller, you will need to reset
the left and right margins for the paragraph.
```

Figure 16-2

Now let's try Method 2.

EXERCISE 16-2

1. Open the file named **quote.wpd.**
2. Select (highlight) the indented paragraph, which is the quote.
3. Choose Layout, Paragraph, and Border/Fill.
4. Choose the Shadow border style from the drop-down list and 10% Fill from the Fill Style drop-down list.
5. Choose OK.
6. Save this file as **quote.bor.** Print one copy and Close the file.

PAGE BORDERS

WordPerfect allows you to create a Page border by placing the Insertion Point anywhere on the page where you want the border to appear. However, the Page Border code **[Pg Border]** will show at the beginning of the page in Reveal Codes. The Page Border code is expandable when highlighted, as are all border codes.

A Page border extends from the top margin to the bottom margin and from the right margin to the left margin. When you create a Page border in WordPerfect, the software automatically allows a little space between the border and the text so that the page is not too crowded and difficult to read.

1. Open the document named **basic.wpd.**
2. Move the Insertion Point to the third paragraph. Choose Layout, Page, and Border/Fill. The Page Border dialog box shown in Figure 16-3 will appear.

EXERCISE 16-3

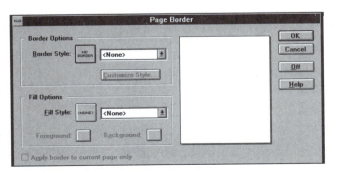

Figure 16-3
Page Border dialog box

LESSON 16 GRAPHICS BORDERS, LINES, AND BOXES **WP201**

3. In this exercise, choose the Single Line border style and a 10% Fill.

4. Because this document consists of only one page, it really doesn't matter whether you select Apply border to current page only. If a document consists of a number of pages and you deselect Apply border to current page only, the border will surround the current page and all subsequent pages in the document. Choose OK.

5. Save this file as **basic.bor** and Print a copy. Close the file.

COLUMN BORDERS

You can also place the Insertion Point anywhere in a column when you want to create a Column border. The border will surround all the columns in your document. The code for the Column border, however, will show in Reveal Codes at the beginning of the document.

In addition to having a border all around the columns, you can select Column Between from the Border Style drop-down list if you want only a vertical separator line between columns, or you can select Column All from the Border Style drop-down list if you want a Column border on the outside edge of the column text and a vertical separator line between columns.

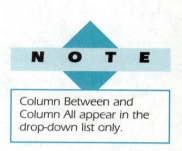

Column Between and Column All appear in the drop-down list only.

EXERCISE 16-4

1. Open the file named **newspap1**.
2. Choose Layout, Columns, and Border/Fill. The Column Border dialog box shown in Figure 16-4 will appear.

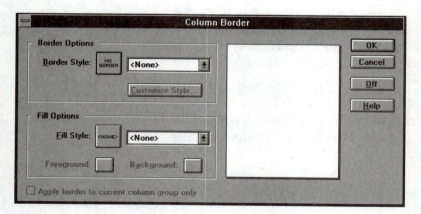

Figure 16-4
Column Border dialog box

3. Click on the Border Style drop-down list and choose Column All.
4. Leave the Fill Style at None.
5. Be sure that Apply border to current column group only is not deselected so that the border will surround columns on the current page and all subsequent pages in the document. Choose OK.
6. View the document before printing it.
7. Print a copy and Save this document as **newspap1.bor**. Close the file.

You can also customize the borders and fill for paragraphs, pages, and columns by clicking on the Customize Style button in each of the dialog boxes. See the Reference manual or User's Guide for information on how to perform the customization.

TURNING OFF A BORDER

There may be times when you do not want a border on a particular page; for example, you may not want a border on a page that contains a complicated graph or a large image. You can turn off the Page border on any page, paragraph, or column in your document through the dialog boxes. You can turn off a border if you:

- Choose Layout and then Page, *or* Paragraph, *or* Column, and choose Border/Fill. Then in the dialog box, choose the command button labeled Off.

DELETING A BORDER

You can delete a Page, Paragraph, or Column border in WordPerfect by deleting the code that represents the border. Follow these steps:

- Choose View and then Reveal Codes, *or* press **Alt+F3**.
- Position the cursor in front of the border code and press **Delete**, *or* drag the code from the Reveal Codes window.

GRAPHICS LINES

You will find the graphics lines capability of WordPerfect useful for enhancing the appearance of a variety of types of documents. They are called graphics lines because they are drawn by WordPerfect and can be printed only on a printer that can print graphics.

You can place horizontal and vertical graphics lines of any length or thickness anywhere on the page. Graphics lines are normally printed as solid black, but you can choose any level of gray shading for any particular line.

Horizontal lines separate text and attract attention. To avoid crowding the text, it is best to create a horizontal line on a blank line. Vertical lines also separate and emphasize text and dress up a page.

ADDING A PREDEFINED VERTICAL OR HORIZONTAL LINE

WordPerfect allows you to place some predefined lines very quickly. All line options such as style, position, length, spacing, thickness, and color are predefined. You can move, size, and edit a predefined line if you want.

Try placing these predefined lines now.

*Open the **wkplace.wpd** file.* To add a predefined horizontal line:

► EXERCISE 16-5

1. Place the Insertion Point on the document LINE where you want to place the line; in this case, between the title and the first paragraph.

2. Choose Graphics and then Horizontal Line. The predefined line will begin at the left margin and extend to the right margin. It will be a single black line of .012" thickness.

To add a predefined vertical line:

3. Place the Insertion Point at the horizontal point where you want the vertical line to appear; in this case, at the beginning of the first paragraph.

4. Choose Graphics and then Vertical Line. The predefined line will begin at the top margin and extend to the bottom margin. It will also be a single black line of .012" thickness.

5. Experiment with placing horizontal and vertical lines in various positions on the page.

6. Do NOT Save this document. Close the file.

N O T E

Before adding lines or any graphics effects, always save a version of your document before you begin. That way, if the result is not as you anticipated, you can always go back to your clean document.

CREATING A CUSTOM GRAPHICS LINE

The Custom Line option lets you create a graphics line with the *exact* style, position, length, spacing, thickness, and color you want.

Beginning with a blank screen:

1. Place the Insertion Point on the page or line where you want to add a graphics line; in this case, on the first line of the blank screen.

2. Choose Graphics and then Custom Line. The Create Graphics Line dialog box shown in Figure 16-5 will appear.

► EXERCISE 16-6

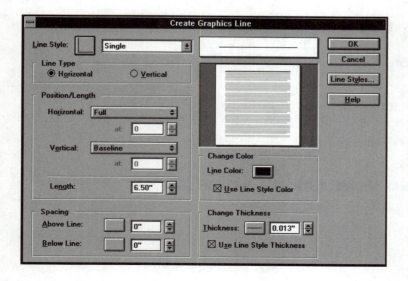

Figure 16-5
Create Graphics Line dialog box

WP204 LESSON 16 GRAPHICS BORDERS, LINES, AND BOXES

Many line options are available through this dialog box. You can specify line style, line type (horizontal or vertical), horizontal or vertical position, length, spacing, color, and line thickness through the Create Graphics Line dialog box. Also, there is a Preview box which allows you to see exactly how the graphics line will appear.

3. Try creating various custom lines through the dialog box, placing the lines wherever you desire. Try the different line options such as style, position, length, and thickness.

4. Use Reveal Codes to become familiar with how the codes appear with different settings. Notice that these are expandable codes that will display more information when you click on them.

5. Use the Page Zoom Full button to see what your file looks like without printing. Save this file with the name **lines1,** but do NOT Close the file.

CUSTOMIZING OR EDITING A GRAPHICS LINE

USING DIALOG BOXES

Just as you can use the dialog box to specify a number of line options as you create a line, you can use the Edit dialog box to customize or edit a graphics line you have already created.

1. Select the graphic line you want by placing the tip of the mouse pointer directly on the line and clicking.

▶ **EXERCISE 16-7**

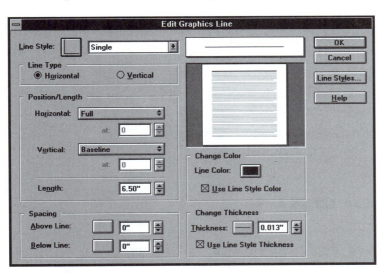

Figure 16-6
Edit Graphics Line dialog box

2. Choose Graphics and then Edit Line. The Edit Graphics Line dialog box shown in Figure 16-6 will appear. You can also click the right mouse button directly on the graphics line, then select Edit Horizontal Line or Edit Vertical Line to move directly to the Edit Graphics Line dialog box.

You will see that this Edit Graphics Line dialog box is essentially the same as the Create dialog box, offering you the same line options from which to choose. The Preview box can be especially helpful as you edit lines.

When you work through the Create Graphics Line dialog box and the Edit Graphics Line dialog box, you can control a number of aspects of a line very exactly. Using the dialog boxes can be somewhat more tedious, however, and in some instances you may prefer to customize or edit your lines using the mouse because it will be easier and faster.

You can also Cut, Copy, and Delete through the QuickMenu available to you when you click on the right mouse button with the mouse directly on the graphics line.

USING THE MOUSE

As you will soon see, the fastest and easiest way to change the length, thickness, or position of a line is to use the mouse—but it is harder to be exact!

Use the following steps to edit a line that is displayed on the screen.

1. Begin by creating a predefined horizontal line.

2. Move the mouse pointer to the line. When the Insertion Point changes to an arrow, click the left mouse button. The line will be selected and will appear as follows:

   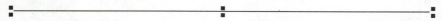

3. Move the mouse pointer to the small black box (a sizing handle) at the lower right corner of the line until the mouse pointer changes to a two-headed diagonal arrow.

4. Click and drag the sizing handle toward the other end of the line to shorten the line. You can also drag the size box down slightly to make the line thicker.

5. When the line reaches the desired thickness and length, release the mouse button. The resulting line should look something like this:

6. Click anywhere on the screen to deselect the line.

CHANGING THE THICKNESS OF A LINE

If you want to change only the thickness of the line, you can use the sizing handles in the middle of the line. Use the sizing handle at the top of the line to increase the width upward or use the sizing handle at the bottom of the line to increase the width downward.

CHANGING THE LENGTH OF A LINE

If you want to change the line length only, move the mouse pointer so that it falls just between the two sizing handles at either end. When the mouse pointer is directly between these handles, it will change to a two-headed horizontal arrow. You can then press the left mouse button and drag to make the line longer or shorter.

MOVING A LINE

To move a graphics line with a mouse, click on the line to select it. Move the mouse pointer to the line itself (not to one of the sizing handles) until it turns into a four-headed arrow. Press the left mouse button and drag the line to the new location. (If necessary, you can even move a line into the left or right margin.) Click anywhere on the screen to deselect the line.

DELETING A LINE

To delete a graphics line, select it and then press **Backspace** or **Delete.**

▶ **EXERCISE 16-9**

Experiment with creating and editing horizontal and vertical lines. Try both the dialog box and mouse methods for editing. Use Reveal Codes and notice how the codes change with your editing changes. When you are familiar with how to create and edit horizontal and vertical lines, clear the screen and continue with the next exercise.

▶ **EXERCISE 16-10**

In this exercise, you will create a newsletter masthead, as shown in Figure 16-7, for a newsletter titled COMPUTER NEWS UPDATE.

COMPUTER NEWS UPDATE

▌ Figure 16-7

1. On a blank screen, key this title in uppercase in an Extra Large font of your choice. Key the title 1" from the top of the page and center it.
2. Create a horizontal line to appear below the title. Use a .18" thickness.
3. Save this file as **newsmast.** Continue with the next exercise.

▶ **EXERCISE 16-11**

1. Place the Insertion Point immediately below the horizontal line in the **newsmast** document. Change the font to Times Roman 12 pt. Insert two blank lines.
2. Insert the file named **newspap1.bor.** Click on Page Zoom Full. The newsletter will have a Column border on the outside of the column text and a vertical separator line between columns because you earlier selected Column All.
3. Save this file as **computns.1.** Print a copy of the first page only and Close the document.

TEXT BOXES

WordPerfect 6.0 for Windows provides a number of different graphics box styles. One of the most useful is the Text Box, which is often used for quotes, sidebars, special announcements, or any other textual information you want to set off from the main document. A Text Box has predefined thick lines on the top and bottom.

▶ **EXERCISE 16-12**

In the following exercise, we will prepare a Text box. First, key the information shown in Figure 16-8 and save the file as **textbox.inf**.

```
Text Boxes serve a useful purpose because they help to
attract the reader's attention to the text.
```

■ Figure 16-8

1. Open the document named **computns.1** and move the Insertion Point to the paragraph in the second column beginning with Other related issues.

2. Click on the Text Box button on the Button Bar, OR choose Graphics and then Text Box. A Text Box is inserted in your document and the Text Box Feature Bar will appear on the screen.

3. The first step is to ensure the Text Box is positioned properly, so click on Position on the Text Box Feature Bar. The Box Position dialog box shown in Figure 16-9 will appear.

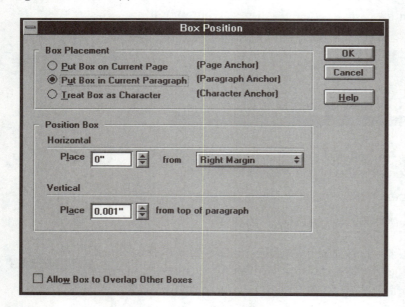

■ Figure 16-9
Box Position dialog box

You have three choices for box placement. You can keep a box next to a specific paragraph or in a certain place on a page, or you can treat a box as a character. In this case, click on Put Box in Current Paragraph. Notice the other options within the dialog box. In this case, you need not use any of them. Click on OK.

4. You could key information in the Text Box, but now you will learn to insert a file containing the information for the box. Choose the Content button on the Text Box Feature Bar. The Box Content dialog box shown in Figure 16-10 will appear.

5. Key the name of the file, **textbox.inf** (specify the disk on which the file is stored), and choose OK. Choose Yes to insert the file into the box.

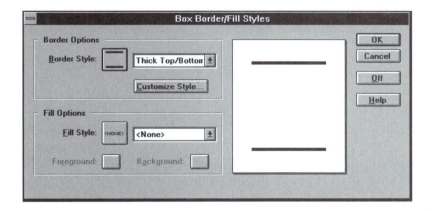

Figure 16-10
Box Content dialog box

6. The last step is to change the border and shade the Text Box. Click on the Border/Fill button on the Feature Bar. The Box Border/Fill Styles dialog box shown in Figure 16-11 will appear. Choose Single from the Border Style list and choose 10% Fill from the Fill Style list. Then choose OK.

Figure 16-11
Box Border/Fill Styles dialog box

7. Choose Close on the Feature Bar. Adjust spacing as necessary in the document.

8. You have now finished the newsletter with a Text Box included. Save the file as **computns.2.** Print a copy of the first page and Close the file.

GRAPHICS BOXES IN REVEAL CODES

When you insert a graphics box into your document, the code which shows in Reveal Codes is an expandable code. When in Reveal Codes, click on the code and you will see much more descriptive information about your graphics box.

You can move and resize a graphics box by selecting it and using the handles in much the same way as you moved and resized graphics lines earlier in this lesson.

DELETING A GRAPHICS BOX

After selecting a graphics box, press **Backspace** or **Delete** to delete it. If you accidentally delete a graphics box, you can immediately choose Edit and then Undo to return it to the screen.

You will find graphics borders, lines, and boxes to be great features! You are likely to find yourself using them for a variety of applications.

REVIEW

TRUE/FALSE

Circle the correct answer.

1. T F You must create a border before you key the text.

2. T F You can create a vertical line between columns, as well as a border on the outside edge of columns, through the Column Border dialog box.

3. T F Graphics lines can be printed only on a printer than can print graphics.

4. T F A WordPerfect Text Box will print with a gray shading default of 10%.

5. T F The major advantage of using the mouse to size and position a Text Box is that it is faster.

6. T F After selecting a graphics box, you can press Backspace or Delete to delete it.

COMPLETION

Fill in the blanks.

1. All of the border codes are _____ when highlighted.

2. The Paragraph border will extend from the _____ _____ to the _____ _____.

3. To avoid crowding the text, it is best to create a _____ line on a blank line.

4. A Text Box has predefined thick lines on the _____ and _____ of the box.

5. If you want to change the line length only, move the _____ _____ so that it falls between the sizing handles at either end.

Understanding Reveal Codes: Open the file named **computns.1**. Find the Column Border code in Reveal Codes and highlight it. Copy it below and explain what it tells you.

REVIEW EXERCISE

In this exercise, you will create the cover sheet shown in Figure 16-12. Perform the following steps:

1. Begin with a clear screen. Change the left margin to 1.5".

2. To place a horizontal line along the top margin, choose Graphics and Custom Line, and then in the dialog box, choose Horizontal. Under Position/Length and Horizontal, click on the arrow and choose Centered. Beside Length, click on the arrow until you get 5.50". You will need to change the Thickness of the line to .1", so move the Insertion Point to Thickness and key `.1"`. Click on OK.

3. To place a similar line across the bottom of your page, again choose Graphics and Custom Line, and then in the dialog box, choose Horizontal and Centered. Change the length to 5.50". Click on the Vertical Baseline, choose Set, and key `10"` to place the line 10" down from the top of the page. Again key the Thickness of line at `.1"`, and click on OK to return to your document screen.

4. Use the Page Zoom Full icon to see how WordPerfect has placed the lines.

5. Press **Enter** ten times.

6. To create the Text Box for the word `Proposal`, choose Graphics and then Text Box, OR click on the Text Box button. The Text Box will appear at the right margin.

7. Choose Layout and then Font. Select Arial, or a similar font and Bold. Change the Relative Size to Extra Large. Click on OK.

8. Center and key `PROPOSAL`. The Text Box will appear at the right margin.

9. Move the box so that it is placed horizontally in the center of the page. Deselect the Text Box. Choose Close on the Feature Bar.

10. Place the Insertion Point after the Text Box and press **Enter** seven times.

11. Since the remainder of the cover sheet is centered text, turn on Center justification. Key the remainder of the text shown in Figure 16-12 on the next page. Use Arial 18 pt. and Bold for the title, including the school and location. Press **Enter** six times and use Arial 14 pt. for the names of the persons to whom the report will go. Press **Enter** two times. Use Arial 10 pt. for the date.

12. When you complete the cover sheet, Save the file with the name **propos1.** Print a copy and then Close the file.

PROPOSAL

COMPUTER LAB SPECIFICATIONS
NORTHSIDE TECHNICAL CENTER
SPRINGFIELD, ILLINOIS

TO
DR. JANET PARKER, PRINCIPAL
DR. CHRIS HAMMITT, SUPERINTENDENT
MEMBERS OF THE BOARD OF EDUCATION

JANUARY 10, 199-

Figure 16-12

LESSON 17

TextArt and Graphics Images

OBJECTIVES

Upon completion of this lesson, you will be able to:

1. Create and edit a TextArt image.
2. Insert graphics images (clip art) into documents.
3. Edit graphics boxes.
4. Edit graphics images.

In this lesson, you will learn about some additional graphics features, TextArt and Graphics Images, which will make your documents more attractive. TextArt will change the appearance of what would otherwise be standard text. Graphics images not only help to make documents more meaningful, but also to make them more attractive. Graphics images can add to the effectiveness of most documents.

CREATING A TEXTART IMAGE

You can enhance the appearance of your documents by using TextArt to modify text and create special images, such as waves, pennants, circles, crescents, or bow ties. TextArt is especially useful to create logos and to call attention to some special text.

1. With a blank screen, choose Graphics and then TextArt, OR click on the TextArt button on the Button Bar. The TextArt in WordPerfect Document dialog box shown in Figure 17-1 will appear.

▶ **EXERCISE 17-1**

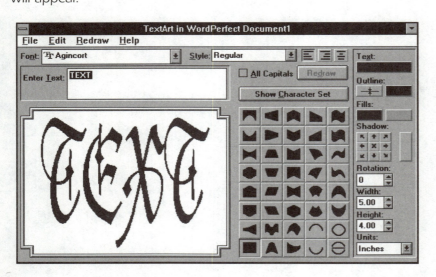

Figure 17-1
TextArt in WordPerfect Document dialog box

2. Across the top of the dialog box are boxes for the image customizing options of Font and Style and three icons showing left, right, or center justified text. Change the font to an Arial font or something similar, but for now, leave the other options as they are.

3. Notice that the word TEXT has already been entered in the Enter Text box. Here is where you key the text you want. You can key up to 58 characters (including spaces) on one, two, or three lines. For now, we will leave the word TEXT.

4. At the right of the Preview screen, below the Show Character Set button, you will see 40 different icons in various shapes. Click on five or six of these shape icons. Notice that as you click on an icon, the word TEXT will assume the shape shown on the icon. Click on the rectangle shape in the lower left corner to change the image back to regular text.

When you move the mouse pointer to a tool, TextArt displays in the message bar (at the bottom of the box) a brief description of the tool.

At the right of the dialog box are various additional options by which you can change the color of the text, use different outline colors and fills, add a shadow, rotate the text, and resize the text in TextArt.

Above Show Character Set are several other options. You can click on All Capitals to change the text to all uppercase quickly. Whether the Redraw option appears dimmed depends on the choice you make in Redraw on the TextArt main menu. If you change Redraw to Manual, the Redraw button activates, and you can choose to show the results of your changes only by clicking on the Redraw button. If you set Redraw to Auto, the text in the Preview box changes automatically each time you make a change.

WP216   LESSON 17   TEXTART AND GRAPHICS IMAGES

By clicking on Show Character Set, you can show or hide, at the bottom of the screen, the character set which goes with the particular font you have currently chosen.

5. Choose File on the TextArt main menu and then Exit & Return to WordPerfect. Choose Yes in reply to the question "Update embedded object(s) in WordPerfect?" to return to your document WITH the TextArt image. As with any other type of graphics, TextArt will be placed at the right margin.

6. Close the file without saving it.

7. Click on the TextArt button again. Key your first name. Experiment with some of the options and fonts to become familiar with how they look. Pick your favorite, Save this file as **t1.**, and Print it. Exit & Return to WordPerfect.

TextArt is a graphics file, even though it looks like text; therefore, it will take longer to save and to print.

In all probability, depending upon the power of the computer on which you are working, you will find it will be slower to work with graphics.

EDITING TEXTART IMAGES

To edit a TextArt image quickly:

- Double-click the left mouse button on the image.

The TextArt in the WordPerfect dialog box will appear showing the image, and you can change it with more exact specifications through the dialog box.

When you are finished, as before, choose File, Exit & Return to WordPerfect, and Yes to return to your document with the edited TextArt image.

You can also use the mouse and click on the image to select the graphic. Sizing handles will appear around the TextArt, as shown in Figure 17-2. As you learned in Lesson 16, you can use these handles to move and size the image quickly and easily—but not as exactly as when you work through the dialog boxes.

Before experimenting with the appearance of any graphics effects, always save a version of your document before you begin. That way, if the result is not as you anticipated, you can always go back to your original document.

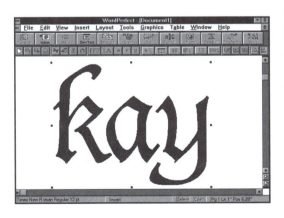

Figure 17-2
TextArt with sizing handles

In this exercise, experiment with the various options available for editing until you feel comfortable with them. Then edit the TextArt file you prepared in Exercise 17-1.

▶ **EXERCISE 17-2**

1. Open the file named **t1** and click on the vertical bar at the right of Shadow. Choose Black and click three times on the right arrow. Save this file with the name **t1**.

2. Now rotate the image 90 degrees. Save this file again with the name **t1**. Print a copy and Close the file.

GRAPHICS IMAGES

WordPerfect has provided you with 134 graphics images as a part of your WordPerfect 6.0 for Windows software. (You can refer to the Reference manual to see these images and their file names. They are not in the User's Guide.) You can also retrieve most graphics images (clip art) from a number of other manufacturers' software, as well as use scanned images or pictures that have been created by a draw program.

There are two ways to add a graphic to a document:

1. You can retrieve a clip art image, a chart, or a drawing directly into a document using the Figure graphics box style, *or*

2. You can create a graphics box using the style you want and then put text, a clip art image, a chart, a drawing, or an equation inside the box.

You can create your own graphics box style or choose from nine different predefined graphics box styles: Figure, Text Box, Equation, Table, User, Button, Watermark, Inline Equation, or OLE Box. Each box has different style options assigned to it, such as border and fill type, corner style, and line color. See the Reference Manual or User's Guide to learn more about the various graphics box styles.

Style options affect the way graphics boxes display on the screen and on a printed document, but they have no effect on what you can put inside each box. You can put text or a graphics image into any graphics box style you want. You can also create a custom box style with the particular border, fill, position, and size options you want.

When you create or edit a graphics box, the Graphics Feature Bar automatically appears below the Power Bar at the top of the screen. The buttons on the Feature Bar automate a number of options that are frequently used to create and edit graphics boxes. You can learn more about what each of these buttons will do when you move the mouse pointer on the button. A brief descriptive message will appear at the top of your screen.

ADDING A GRAPHICS IMAGE DIRECTLY INTO A DOCUMENT

Now you will use the Figure box style to retrieve an image created in WordPerfect format with the extension **.wpg** directly into a document.

EXERCISE 17-3

1. Open the document named **newspap.1.**
2. Place the Insertion Point where you want the graphics box to appear; in this case, at the beginning of the second paragraph. The box will be inserted flush right and will be aligned with the top of the paragraph.
3. Choose Graphics and then Figure, OR click on the Figure button on the Button Bar. The Insert Image dialog box shown in Figure 17-3 will appear. Notice the list of images in .wpg files available to you. You can key the name of the file you want or scroll through the list and click on the file name.

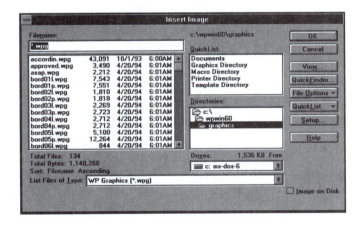
Figure 17-3
Insert Image dialog box

4. Click on the file **world.wpg** and choose View. You will see the image, as shown in Figure 17-4, in the lower right corner of the dialog box.
5. Choose OK. The graphics image you have chosen will appear where you indicated it should be placed in the document and the Graphics Feature Bar will appear.
6. Deselect the graphics image.
7. Save this file as **newspap.wld,** but do not Close it.

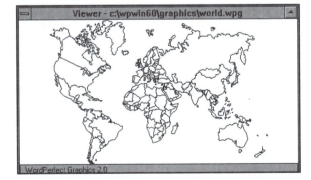
Figure 17-4
world.wpg

LESSON 17 TEXTART AND GRAPHICS IMAGES **WP219**

The buttons on the Graphics Feature Bar will help you to perform various actions in regard to the graphics box and graphics image. A number of these actions can be performed more easily and quickly with the mouse, but they will not be as exact as when you use a dialog box.

EDITING GRAPHICS BOXES

CAPTION

WordPerfect enables you to add captions easily to the graphics boxes you create. Captions are an effective way to add explanatory information about the box contents.

In this exercise, you will learn to add a caption to the graphics box you created in the last exercise.

1. Select the graphics box containing the world by clicking within the box.

2. Click the right mouse button on the graphics box, and then select Create Caption. Immediately the caption Figure 1 will appear at the bottom of the graphics box.

3. Since you do not want a figure and number in the caption, press **Backspace** to delete the number style. Do this now. (If you delete the number style by mistake sometime, you can choose Edit and then Undo.)

4. Key the caption text `Computers are used worldwide today.` The Caption Editor functions just like the document window. You can edit text using regular WordPerfect features. For example, you can change fonts and line spacing and you can cut, copy, and paste.

5. When you are finished, choose Close from the Feature Bar to return to your document.

6. Save this file as **newspap.cap,** but do not Close the file.

7. See the explanation below and experiment with moving the caption now. Close the file without saving it.

You can change the position of a caption by clicking on the Caption button on the Feature Bar and, when the Box Caption dialog box appears, selecting whatever Caption Position option you want. Notice the other caption options, including Rotation, available to you, as shown in Figure 17-5 on the next page.

WP220   LESSON 17   TEXTART AND GRAPHICS IMAGES

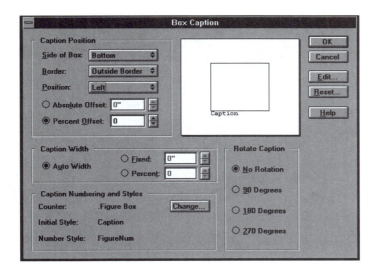

Figure 17-5
Box Caption dialog box

CONTENT

By clicking on the Content button on the Feature Bar, the Box Content dialog box will appear. Through this box, you can specify exactly where the image should appear within the graphics box.

POSITION

When you click on the Position button, the Box Position dialog box shown in Figure 17-6 will appear. On this box, you can indicate the exact position where you wish to locate the box and image on the page. You can also move the graphics box similar to the way you moved a graphics line in the last lesson. Select the graphic and move the mouse pointer to the graphic itself until it turns into a four-headed arrow. Press the left mouse button and drag the image to the new location.

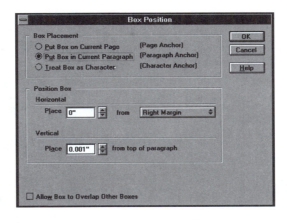

Figure 17-6
Box Position dialog box

SIZE

When you click on the Size button, the Box Size dialog box shown in Figure 17-7 will appear. Through this box, you can specify the width and height of a graphics box. You can also size the graphics box by selecting the graphic and dragging the handles to enlarge or decrease the size of the graphics box.

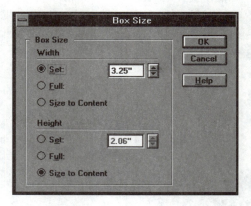

Figure 17-7
Box Size dialog box

BORDER/FILL

When you click on the Border/Fill button on the Feature Bar, the Box Border/Fill Styles dialog box will appear. (See Figure 17-8.)

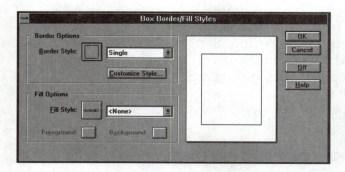

Figure 17-8
Box Border/Fill Styles dialog box

In this exercise, you will enhance the appearance of your graphics box to make it more noticeable to the reader.

▶ **EXERCISE 17-5**

1. Select the graphics box.
2. Click on the Border/Fill button.
3. Change the Border Style to Thick.
4. Change the Fill to 10%. Click on OK.
5. Click on the Close button to return to the document. You will see how the appearance has been enhanced immediately.
6. Save this document as **newsgrph.b&f.** Print a copy and Close the file.

Although in this lesson you are learning about all of the graphics features on the Feature Bar, you would not usually use all of them. Instead, you would pick and choose which features are most appropriate to what you are trying to achieve.

Graphics take longer to print than text, so be prepared to wait a little longer.

WRAP

You can specify how you want the document text to flow around or through a graphics box. You can also choose to have document text follow the contour of an image.

In this exercise, you will learn how you can have the document text follow the contour of an image.

1. Open the file named **basic.**

2. Just for fun, we will insert a cat into it. Move the Insertion Point to the beginning of the second paragraph and click on the Figure icon on the Button Bar. Select the graphic **housecat.wpg** and click on OK to bring it into a Figure Box. The graphics box will appear in your document at the right side. (Although the graphic will show in color on a color monitor, it cannot be printed in color unless you have a color printer.)

3. Move the Insertion Point inside the box until you see the four-headed arrow, and then move the graphic to the approximate center of the page horizontally. Save this file as **basic.cat** so that you have a clean graphics file should you need it.

4. Click on the Wrap button on the Feature Bar. The Wrap Text dialog box shown in Figure 17-9 will appear.

Figure 17-9
Wrap Text dialog box

5. Experiment with clicking on the various options and combinations in the Wrapping Type and Wrap Text Around lists. Choose OK and you will immediately see the results. Which looks the best? As you will notice, some make it hard for the reader to follow the text.

6. Move the cat to the right and in the Wrap Text dialog box, choose Contour and Left Side. Click on Close on the Feature Bar.

7. Save this file as **basiccat.con.** Print a copy and Close the file.

EDITING GRAPHICS IMAGES

IMAGE TOOLS

The Image Tools palette provides you with several options for working with graphics images. When you click on the Tools button on the Feature Bar, WordPerfect will display the Image Tools palette shown in Figure 17-10. You can learn what each of the tools will do by placing the mouse pointer on the icon to see a brief description in the Title Bar at the top of the screen. You will learn how to obtain a mirrored image and how to move the image within a box.

Figure 17-10
Image Tools palette

▶ **EXERCISE 17-7**

Perform the following steps in order:

1. On a blank screen, select the Figure button.
2. Insert the graphics image named **jockey.wpg**.
3. Click on the Tools button on the Graphics Feature Bar.
4. The two tools icons on the sixth row are used to obtain a mirrored image. The icon on the left will mirror the image on the horizontal axis, while the icon on the right will mirror the image on the vertical axis. In this instance, click the left icon so that the jockey is reversed horizontally.
5. By clicking on the Hand icon in the top row, you can move the image within the graphics box. You can place the hand on the image and move the image however you want to within the box. Try moving the image now.
6. Once you have moved an image, you may want to resize the box. You can do that by clicking on the Arrow icon, which enables the mouse for box movement. Then you can quickly size the box with the mouse or choose the Position button on the Feature Bar to do so more exactly.
7. Resize the box so that it is about 4" x 4" and move the box so that it is centered on the page horizontally. Close the image tools box and Feature Bar.
8. Save the file as **jockey.1**. Print a copy and Close the file.

ROTATING IMAGES

Another one of the Image Tools is for rotation; it is the first icon in the first row of the Image Tools palette. You can rotate an image within the graphics box by using the Rotation tool.

In this exercise, you will learn how to rotate an image to give a different look to your graphic.

▶ **EXERCISE 17-8**

1. On a blank screen, click on the Figure button.
2. Insert the graphics image named **horse-j.wpg**.

WP224   LESSON 17   TEXTART AND GRAPHICS IMAGES

3. Click on the Tools button on the Graphics Feature Bar.

4. Click on the Rotate icon, the first icon in the first row. Small double handles appear in the corners of the image.

5. Move the mouse over one of the new handles appearing INSIDE the graphics box until the double-headed arrow appears.

6. Click and drag on these handles until you become familiar with how they work to rotate the image.

7. Rotate the horse until it looks like the image in Figure 17-11.

8. Save the file as **horse.rot.** Print a copy and Close the file.

■ **Figure 17-11**
Rotated horse

The WordPerfect 6.0 for Windows software includes many other features for creating, manipulating, and editing graphics, including WordPerfect Draw and Charting. See your Reference Manual or User's Guide for more information on how to use these additional features.

For additional practice with graphics:

▶ **EXERCISE 17-9**

1. Key the text in Figure 17-12, referring to the lessons on graphics as needed.

2. Place the graphics images **accordin.wpg, piano.wpg,** and **trumpet.wpg** (all of which ship with WordPerfect 6.0 for Windows) in figure boxes within the document.

Be creative and use the graphics features available in WordPerfect with which you have become familiar. Experiment with different fonts and different font sizes, graphics lines, borders, fills, TextArt, graphics boxes, and images to create as attractive a notice as you can.

3. Save this file as **musicles.fly.** Print a copy and Close the file.

```
Private and Group Music Lessons
After School and on Saturdays
Accordian, Trumpet, Trombone, Guitar and Many Other
Instruments
You Name It!

We offer Suzuki piano lessons, as well as lessons on
all other types of instruments.  Special rates are
available for lessons for three or more children
per week.

We have degrees in music education and we know how to
teach your children!

Miles and Keiko O'Brien, Instructors
Call 555-5000 for more information today!
```

■ **Figure 17-12**

REVIEW

TRUE/FALSE

Circle the correct answer.

1. T   F   Figure Boxes can be sized or moved in the same way as Text Boxes.
2. T   F   You can learn more about what each of the buttons on the Graphics Feature Bar will do when you place the mouse pointer on it.
3. T   F   Graphics with the .wpg extension have been created in WordPerfect graphics format.
4. T   F   Regardless of the shape of the graphics image, the text will always flow around the graphics box.
5. T   F   The Image Tools palette provides a number of special tools for working with graphics images.

COMPLETION

Fill in the blanks.

1. _____ is useful to modify text and to put it into unusual shapes.
2. You must _____ a graphics line or box for the sizing handles to appear.
3. To move and size graphics lines and boxes quickly, click on the _____ _____ .
4. Actions performed with the mouse can be performed more easily and quickly, but they will not be as _____ as those set in a dialog box.
5. A _____ image is reversed horizontally so that it is facing the opposite direction from the original.

Understanding Reveal Codes:

1. Open the file named **newspap.wld.** Find the Box code in Reveal Codes and highlight it. Copy it below.

2. Open the file named **newsgrph.b&f.** Find the Box code in Reveal Codes and highlight it. Copy it below.

3. Compare the two codes and explain the differences.

4. A visual examination of the **newspap.b&f** document tells you that there is a caption and that the box has a border and fill. If you were to decide to remove these additions, how would you go about doing this?

LESSON 17 TEXTART AND GRAPHICS IMAGES **WP227**

LESSON 18

Macros

OBJECTIVES

Upon completion of this lesson, you will be able to:

1. Create or record a macro.
2. Play a macro.
3. Edit a macro.
4. Use WordPerfect macros.

You will find it worthwhile to learn about macros because they are shortcuts that help you be more productive! A **macro** is a series of commands and menu selections in a file that can be replayed by a few keystrokes or by a mouse click. You will find macros especially useful to perform quickly some of those tasks you perform over and over.

In a classroom or laboratory, you must save your macros on your own disk. Do NOT store your macro on the hard disk or network.

CREATING OR RECORDING A MACRO

Creating or recording a macro is somewhat like making an audiotape on your cassette player. First, you give your recording a name or you name the macro. The next step is to create or record what you want to be recorded. Finally, you play what you have recorded. Perform the steps carefully in the following exercise to learn how to create a macro for a complimentary close that is used regularly.

You should begin with a blank screen, and then:

Figure 18-1
Record Macro dialog box

1. Choose Tools, Macro, and Record. The Record Macro dialog box shown in Figure 18-1 will appear.

2. Key the drive letter on which the macro is to be saved (`a:` or `b:`) and key the name of the macro to be recorded; in this case, `Close`. WordPerfect automatically assigns a **.wcm** extension to the file name. Whenever you see a file with the extension **.wcm,** you will know that it is a WordPerfect macro.

3. Choose Record to begin recording the macro. You will be returned to the blank document window. The message "Macro Record" will display on the Status Bar while you are recording the macro.

4. Use WordPerfect as you normally would to create the following closing:

```
Sincerely,

(Leave 3 blank lines here)

Your Name
President
```

5. To stop recording, choose Tools, Macro, and Record.

6. Close the file.

As you can see, it is quite easy to record a macro to do lots of things for you. While recording a macro, you can use the mouse to select menu commands and dialog box options, size a document window, scroll through open document windows, or close a document window. However, when recording a macro, you cannot use the mouse pointer to scroll the text with the Scroll Bars, move the Insertion Point through the text, or Select text. You must use the keyboard to move through the text. To Select text, you must click the Insertion Point immediately before the first character you want to select, and then press the Select key (**F8**).

PLAYING A MACRO

Playing a macro will repeat the actions that you recorded every time you play the macro.

To play the complimentary close you just recorded:

1. Choose Tools, Macro, and Play. The Play Macro dialog box shown in Figure 18-2 on the next page will appear.

2. Key the drive and the name of the macro you want to play; in this case, **close.wcm.** Then choose Play or press **Enter.**

▶ **EXERCISE 18-1**

▶ **EXERCISE 18-2**

A faster and easier method to play this macro is to choose Tools and Macro. At the bottom of the Macros drop-down menu, you will see the name of the last macro you played or recorded. You can highlight and select this macro very quickly.

Figure 18-2
Play Macro dialog box

EDITING A MACRO

Sometimes you will want to change a macro after you have recorded it. You do not need to do it over. You can simply edit it.

To edit the complimentary close you recorded in Exercise 18-1:

EXERCISE 18-3

1. Choose Tools, Macro, and Edit.
2. Key the drive and the name of the macro you want to edit; in this case, **close.wcm.** Notice the appearance of the macro. WordPerfect automatically inserts the Application command when you record a macro. The text you have keyed will be preceded by the word Type and will be placed in parentheses and quotation marks. Note the hard returns you inserted.
3. Now key new commands or edit existing commands or text. In this case, change the closing to read Sincerely yours, and put your instructor's name in place of your name.
4. When you are through editing, click on the Options button on the Macro Feature Bar and choose Close Macro.
5. Choose Yes to save the macro and Close the document window.

You can learn more about the macro commands by referring to the Help menu or to your Reference Manual or User's Guide.

You can also edit a macro that you have on your disk by opening it into a document window, making your changes, and saving it to the same file. The Macro Feature Bar will not appear, however.

USING WORDPERFECT MACROS

WordPerfect comes with a library of macros that have already been created to perform a variety of tasks. When in the Play Macro dialog box, you can press **F4** or **Alt+Down** to see a list of macros. If you want more information about what each of these macros will do, you can print a list of the macros and descriptions of what they will do. Let's do that now.

LESSON 18   MACROS   **WP231**

1. Choose <u>H</u>elp and then <u>M</u>acros, and click on Shipping Macros in the left column. The list of macros shown in Figure 18-4 will appear.
2. Click on Print on the Button Bar and then on Close.

EXERCISE 18-4

Shipping Macros

ADRS2MRG.WCM	Copies the address book (for automated templates) into a merge data file.
ALLFONTS.WCM	Creates a document listing the name and some sample text from every font available to the current printer.
AUTOFILL.WCM	Used by the ExpressDocs shipping templates to automate the template fillin process.
CAPITAL.WCM	Capitalizes the first letter of the current word.
CLOSEALL.WCM	Closes all documents currently open and prompts to save any that have been modified.
CLPBRD.WCM	Opens the Windows Clipboard.
CTRLSFTF.WCM	Prompts for FROM and TO values for the equation editor.
DROPCAPS.WCM	Changes the first letter in a paragraph to a large drop cap.
EXPNDALL.WCM	Expands all abbreviations in the document in one step.
ENDFOOT.WCM	Converts endnotes to footnotes in document or selected text.
FILESTMP.WCM	Places the filename and path of the current document in a header or footer.
FONTDN.WCM	Decreases the font size of the selected text by two points.
FONTUP.WCM	Increases the font size of the selected text by two points.
FOOTEND.WCM	Converts footnotes to endnotes in document or selected text.
GOTODOS.WCM	Opens a DOS window.
LINENUM.WCM	Positions insertion point at a specified line and character for debugging macros.
PAGEXOFY.WCM	Places "Page x of y pages" (or other formats) in specified position on paper.
PARABRK.WCM	Inserts graphical paragraph breaks between paragraphs.
PGBORDER.WCM	Creates decorative page borders with WordPerfect graphics.
REVERSE.WCM	Creates white text on black background (or other color options as set by the user) in document text or tables.
SAVEALL.WCM	Saves all documents currently open and prompts to save any that have been modified.
SQCONFIG.WCM	Configures the Smart Quotes utility.
SQTOGGLE.WCM	Turns on and off the Smart Quotes utility.
TRANSPOSE.WCM	Transposes the two characters preceding the insertion point.
WATERMRK.WCM	Prompts for text or watermark graphic that will be placed in watermark (centered vertically and horizontally).

■ Figure 18-4

Look over the list to get an idea of what macros come with your WordPerfect software. Keep this list available and look it over now and then. You surely will find some of these useful in the future; for example, you may find the **closeall.wcm** and **saveall.wcm** macros particularly useful when you are in a hurry. Now let's try one of the others.

▶ **EXERCISE 18-5**

1. Open the file named **docassem.ftn.**
2. Play the macro named **footend.wcm.** Look over your document. This macro should have converted the footnotes to endnotes.
3. Close the file.

Wasn't that wonderful? If you want the flexibility of trying either endnotes or footnotes, it's great to have macros available. Now let's try another.

▶ **EXERCISE 18-6**

1. Open the file named **docassem.end.**
2. This time look at the macro by choosing Tools, Macro, and Edit, keying the name **endfoot.wcm.,** and clicking on Edit. You can appreciate this macro even more because you can see how complicated this was to record. Click on Options and then on Close Macro.
3. Now play the macro named **endfoot.wcm.** Look over your document. This macro should have converted the endnotes to footnotes.
4. Close the file.

CAUTION: Do not save any changes to the macro!

WATERMARK

A watermark can be used to add a drawing, logo, or some large text as a graphic to appear behind the printed document text. Word-Perfect provides quite a group of Watermark macros that can be fun to use! We will try one now.

▶ **EXERCISE 18-7**

1. Be sure you have a blank screen.
2. Choose Tools, Macro, and Play, and press **F4.** Double-click on **watermrk.wcm** and choose Play.
3. When you are prompted for the Watermark options, click on OK. A list of graphics watermarks will appear. Look over what is available. Notice that you can preview any of these.
4. Highlight **For your Eyes Only** and click on OK. The watermark will appear. Notice that the Insertion Point is positioned over the watermark because watermarks are always printed behind the printed document text.
5. Insert the file named **quote.wpd** and Print a copy. Save this file as **watermk.qte.** Close the file.

Macros are indeed wonderful, but they can be complicated. If you are interested in learning more about macros, you can study macros through the Help menu and in your Reference Manual or User's Guide.

REVIEW

TRUE/FALSE

Circle the correct answer.

1. T F The first step in creating or recording a macro is to name it.

2. T F You may be limited in your use of the mouse when you are recording a macro.

3. T F The fastest way to play a macro which you just recorded is to click on he last macro name listed at the bottom of the Macros menu.

4. T F One way of editing a macro that is on your disk is to open it into a document window, make your changes, and then save it to the same file.

5. T F There is no way to know what a watermark will look like until you print it.

COMPLETION

Fill in the blank.

1. A macro is a series of _____ and _____ _____ in a file that can be replayed by a few key strokes or by a mouse click.

2. The file name extension for macros is _____.

3. When in the _____ _____ dialog box, you can press F4 or Alt+Down Arrow to see a list of the macros.

4. You can learn more about macros by looking in the Reference Manual or User's Guide or by choosing _____ from the Help menu.

5. A watermark will always be printed _____ the text of the document.

WP234   LESSON 18   MACROS

Understanding Macros: You learned about the macros shipped with WordPerfect by choosing Help and Macros. In addition to Shipping Macros, list the other macro topics available to you through Help.

REVIEW EXERCISES

Now as a quick review, record a macro containing:

> Your Name
> Street Address
> City, State and ZIP

Save this macro as **name.**

Play another watermark of your choice and place it behind a document of your choice.

Print a copy and close the file.

Culminating Project
Creating a Flyer

In this exercise, you will use many of the WordPerfect 6.0 for Windows features that you have learned about throughout this Quick Course. Follow the instructions below to create the flyer shown in Figure CP-1. Try to make this project look like the example without referring back to the lessons. Adjust font size, spacing, and format as necessary.

1. Start with a blank document screen.
2. Insert **pointout.wpg** in a Figure box. Move it to the upper left-hand corner of the page and size it to approximately 1" x 1".
3. Key the title in Eurostile-WP 24 pt. (or something similar), and then change to 12 pt.
4. Create a horizontal line below the title which is .05" thick.
5. Change your font to Times New Roman (or something similar).
6. Space down so your Insertion Point is at the left margin below the graphic, and define two evenly spaced Newspaper columns.
7. Place a border around the columns and a vertical line between columns.
8. Turn on Hyphenation and Full justify the text.
9. Key the text of the flyer, making sure to bold the subtitles and italicize where necessary.
10. Create a table at the end of the text. Use Arial 8 pt. (or something similar).
11. Justify the cells as shown. Make sure to shade the top row.
12. Run the Speller.
13. Save this file with the name **postal.** Print a Copy and Close the file.

Check Your Knowledge about The United States Postal Service

WHAT IS POSTAL AUTOMATION? The answer is *changing technology*. Automation is the term used to refer to computerized mail processing. Computerized processing is not only many times faster than manual or mechanized sorting methods, but also a much more efficient, economical, and accurate process that provides mail service improvements from collection to delivery.

WHAT IS AUTOMATION'S ROLE IN THE MAIL FLOW? At the central post office, all mail is sorted by size first. Letters over a certain height and thickness are removed from the mailstream. The remaining letters travel by conveyor belt to a *Facer-Canceler* machine. As each letter enters the machine, detectors look for postage. When a valid form of postage is detected, the letter is:

1. Postmarked: A fluorescent circle impression is applied, indicating the post office and date of receipt for processing.
2. Canceled: A fluorescent bar impression is applied to a portion of the postage so it cannot be reused.
3. Directed: To an acceptance tray.

The Facer-Canceler also looks for the FIM (Facing Identification Mark) to identify pre-barcoded pieces. Prebarcoded pieces bypass several handlings for more efficient processing.

From the Facer-Canceler, letters are sent to the *Optical Character Reader* (OCR). The OCR has the capability of reading up to five lines of address information! Information is verified by a computer. The ZIP code or ZIP+4 code is sprayed on the letter in the form of a *bar code* by the OCR's printer.

Barcoded letters are sent to the *Bar Code Sorter* (BCS). The BCS reads the bar codes and sends letters to their appropriate channels for delivery. The BCS can read and identify an OCR-applied bar code or a mailer-applied bar code which is part of the address block. Prebarcoding by the mailer allows the mail to bypass the OCR.

Letters that cannot be successfully processed on the OCR are sent to the *Multi Position Letter Sorting Machine* (MPLSM), which is not part of automation. The MPLSM requires operators to read and interpret the address information on a letter. Prior to the deployment of the OCR and BCS, all machinable mail was processed on the MPLSM.

There are substantial differences in cost effectiveness, depending upon the system used. Note the differences in the table below.

	OCR/BCS	MPLSM	MANUAL
Average number of letters per clerk-hour	18,000	2,118	1,000
Number of clerks	2/minimum training required	17/specialized training required	1/specialized training required

Figure CP-1

Appendix A
Customizing Options

This is for your information, but do *not* try to do this in your classroom or laboratory.

WordPerfect 6.0 for Windows lets you customize your interface in such ways as adding or deleting features on menus and Button Bars, modifying the Power Bar to include functions you use most, and specifying changes to the Ruler Bar and Status Bar. You can customize almost everything that you can see in WordPerfect by using Preferences. Through Preferences, you can set options that are in effect each time you start WordPerfect.

BUTTON BAR

SELECTING A BUTTON BAR

You can change the Button Bar by choosing File and then Preferences, and by double-clicking on the Button Bar icon. A Button Bar Preferences dialog box will appear, containing a list of 12 predefined Button Bars that are available through WordPerfect 6.0 for Windows or 15 available through 6.0a. (See Figure A-1.) Highlight a Button Bar, choose Select, and then choose Close.

Figure A-1
Button Bar Preferences dialog box

For example, if you do many layout changes or font changes daily, you would find it worthwhile to highlight and select the Layout or Font Button Bars. Look over what is available to you, either as a complete Button Bar or separate buttons, because you will learn how to create your own Button Bar.

Note that you can also click the right mouse button anywhere on a displayed Button Bar to obtain a QuickMenu, and then select a new Button Bar. (See Figure A-2 on the next page.)

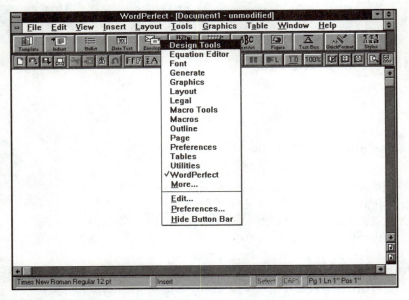

Figure A-2
Button Bar QuickMenu

DISPLAYING (OR HIDING) A BUTTON BAR

Choose View and then Button Bar, *or* choose the Button Bar icon on the Power Bar. If Button Bar is not checked, by choosing it, you can display it; if Button Bar is checked, by choosing it, you can hide it.

CHANGING THE POSITION OF THE BUTTON BAR

By default, the Button Bar is displayed horizontally at the top of the screen, under the main menu. You can change the location of a Button Bar on the screen by choosing File, Preferences, Button Bar, and Options.

The Button Bar Options dialog box will appear. (See Figure A-3.)

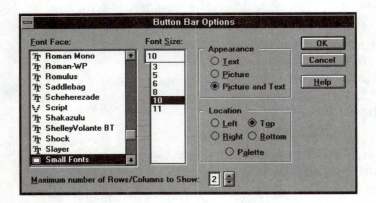

Figure A-3
Button Bar Options dialog box

You can choose a Location of left, right, top, bottom, or palette. Choose OK, Close, and then Close again to return to a blank screen.

WP240   APPENDIX A   CUSTOMIZING OPTIONS

You can also place the pointer on a button separator or blank area of the Button Bar so that the pointer changes to a Hand icon. Then drag the Button Bar to the top, bottom, left, or right edge of the screen or anywhere in the document window. When in the document window, the Button Bar is converted to a palette of buttons.

CHANGING THE BUTTON STYLE

WordPerfect can display Button Bar buttons with text and pictures (the default), or with pictures only or text only. Buttons formatted with the Picture option take up the least space on horizontal Button Bars; the Text option takes the least space on vertical Button Bars. Switching to text only or pictures only saves screen space and displays more buttons on screen without the need for scrolling. To change the button style, Choose File, Preferences, Button Bar, and Options, *or*

Click the right mouse button on the Button Bar to display the QuickMenu, and choose Preferences and then Options. The Button Bar Options dialog box will appear. (See Figure A-3 on the previous page.) Under Appearance, you can choose Text, Picture, or Picture and Text. Choose OK, Close, and then Close again (if necessary) to return to the editing screen.

CUSTOMIZING A BUTTON BAR

You can customize your own buttons on a Button Bar by repositioning buttons from other Button Bars and by assigning program functions, keystrokes, or macros to buttons.

To edit a Button Bar, choose File, Preferences, and Button Bar.

In the Button Bar Preferences dialog box, choose Copy. In the Copy Button Bars dialog box (See Figure A-4.) Choose a Button Bar from the Select Button Bars to Copy box and click on Copy.

In the Overwrite/New Name dialog box shown in Figure A-5 on the next page, key a new name for the copied Button Bar in the Object box. Choose OK.

Figure A-4
Copy Button Bar(s) dialog box

WordPerfect will then list the copy of the Button Bar in the Available Button Bars list box, where you can now select it (or the copied Button Bar) and choose Edit to customize.

Figure A-5
Overwrite/New Name dialog box

MOVING BUTTON BAR BUTTONS

You can move the buttons on the Button Bar. You can decide whether you want to place the buttons you use most frequently at the left end of the bar or in the center. You can group buttons by adding spacers between the groups. To add more buttons on the Button Bar, choose File, Preferences, Button Bar, and Edit, *or* click the Button Bar with the right mouse button to display the QuickMenu, and then choose Edit.

WordPerfect will display the Button Bar Editor dialog box. (See Figure A-6.)

Figure A-6
Button Bar Editor dialog box

With the Button Bar Editor displayed, drag a button to a new location. To insert a spacer between buttons, drag the spacer symbol at the bottom of the dialog box between two buttons on the Button Bar and release the mouse button.

To delete a button, drag it off the Button Bar, *or* click with the right mouse button, and choose Delete. Choose OK, Close, and Close to return to the editing screen.

BUTTON BARS PROVIDED BY WORDPERFECT

WordPerfect 6.0a for Windows provides the following Button Bars from which you can choose in the Button Bar Preferences dialog box: Design Tools, Equation Editor, Font, Generate, Graphics, Layout, Legal, Macro Tools, Macros, Outline, Page, Preferences, Tables, Utilities, and WordPerfect. (The WordPerfect Button Bar is the default which ships installed with WordPerfect. See Figures A-7 through A-21.) When you click on More, you can choose from the WordPerfect 5.2 Button Bar, as well as any you have customized.

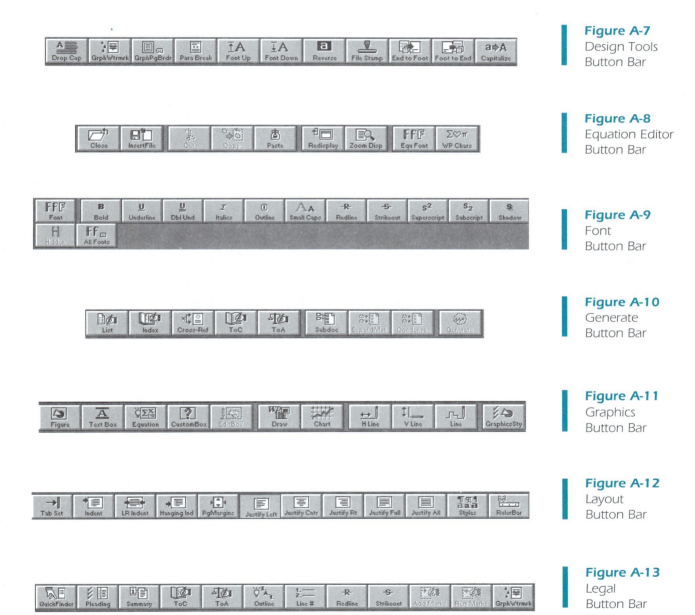

Figure A-7
Design Tools
Button Bar

Figure A-8
Equation Editor
Button Bar

Figure A-9
Font
Button Bar

Figure A-10
Generate
Button Bar

Figure A-11
Graphics
Button Bar

Figure A-12
Layout
Button Bar

Figure A-13
Legal
Button Bar

APPENDIX A CUSTOMIZING OPTIONS **WP243**

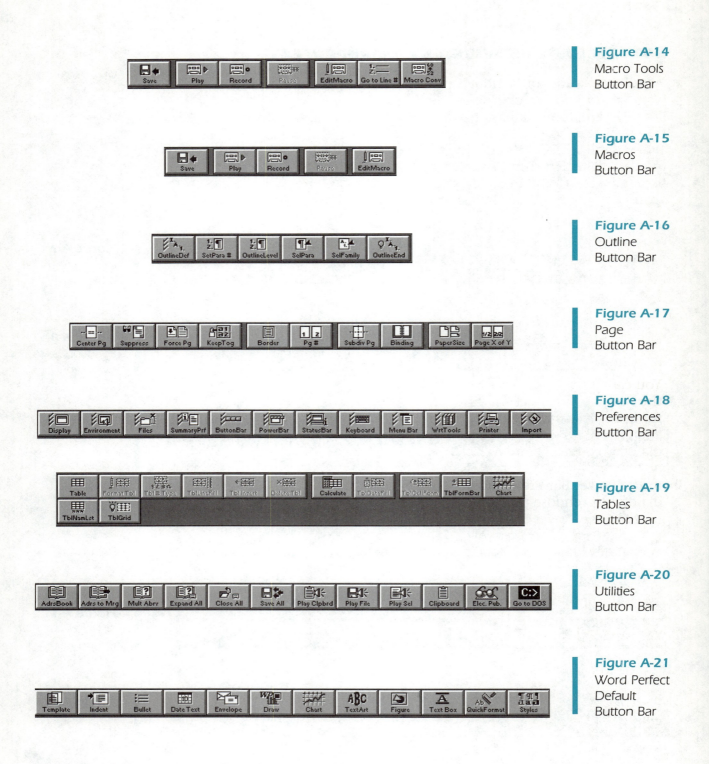

Figure A-14 Macro Tools Button Bar

Figure A-15 Macros Button Bar

Figure A-16 Outline Button Bar

Figure A-17 Page Button Bar

Figure A-18 Preferences Button Bar

Figure A-19 Tables Button Bar

Figure A-20 Utilities Button Bar

Figure A-21 Word Perfect Default Button Bar

Note that some are not full and there is room for you to add other buttons easily. Also, the standard Button Bar for WordPerfect 6.0 for Windows includes a button for Merge instead of a button for Template, which is included in version 6.0a.

POWER BAR

The Power Bar is the row of small buttons at the top of the document window. The Power Bar lets you access the features you use in every task. You can choose from 81 common tasks to add to your Power Bar.

You can create only Power Bar buttons that apply commands from a list, and you cannot move the Power Bar to a new location on the screen.

HIDING AND VIEWING THE POWER BAR

You can turn the Power Bar on and off in three ways:

1. Choose View and then Power Bar, *or*
2. Click the right mouse button anywhere on the Power Bar, and choose Hide Power Bar, *or*
3. Choose View and then Hide Bars.

You can customize both the Font Face and Font Size buttons on the Power Bar so that their pop-up menus display the fonts and font sizes you use most frequently by choosing File, Preferences, and Power Bar. WordPerfect will display the Power Bar Preferences dialog box. (See Figure A-22.)
or
in the Power Bar Preferences dialog box, choose the Fonts button. The Power Bar Font/Size Lists dialog box will appear. (See Figure A-23 on the next page.) Select the appropriate check boxes for the fonts and font sizes you want displayed on the Font Face and Font Size buttons' pop-up menus. Choose OK to return to the Power Bar Preferences dialog box.

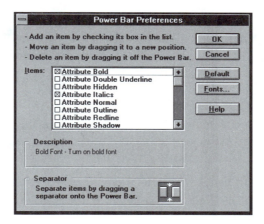

Figure A-22
Power Bar Preferences dialog box

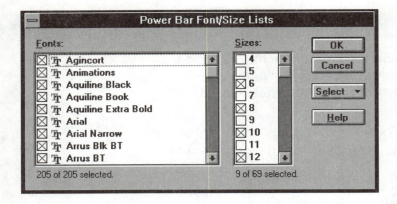

Figure A-23
Power Bar Font/Size Lists dialog box

ADDING, MOVING, AND DELETING POWER BAR BUTTONS

Choose File, Preferences, and Power Bar, *or*

Click the Power Bar anywhere with the right mouse button and choose Preferences. WordPerfect will display the Power Bar Preferences dialog box shown in Figure A-22 on the previous page.

Note that before you can add a button, you may need to delete a button to make room for it. To *delete* a button, drag the button off the Power Bar while the Power Bar Preferences dialog box is displayed.

To *add* a button to the Power Bar, check a box in the Items list. Your changes are reflected in the Power Bar. Some commands provide a choice between a combo box and a pop-up box; for example, Font Size combo box or Font Size pop-up box. A combo box, when checked, displays a list that enables you to select a size while you hold down the mouse button. A pop-up box displays a list that remains on screen after you release the mouse button; you can scroll a pop-up list with the mouse by using scroll arrows.

To *move* a button, drag the button to the new location while the Power Bar Preferences dialog box is displayed.

To add a space between buttons, drag the spacer symbol to the desired location on the Power Bar.

To restore the default Power Bar buttons, choose Default.

Choose OK to return to the document window.

MENU BAR

If you use some features frequently and others not at all, you may find it useful to create your own menus. The Menu Bar Editor lets you move, delete, and add features to all the pull-down menus or customize any of the pull-down menus on the Menu Bar.

CREATING OR EDITING A MENU

Choose File and Preferences, and then double-click on the Menu Bar icon. The Menu Bar Preferences dialog box will appear. (See Figure A-24.)

Figure A-24
Menu Bar Preferences dialog box

Choose Create; the Create Menu Bar dialog box will appear. (See Figure A-25.)

Figure A-25
Create Menu Bar dialog box

Key a name for your Menu Bar and choose OK. The Menu Bar Editor dialog box will appear. (See Figure A-26 on the next page.)

APPENDIX A CUSTOMIZING OPTIONS   **WP247**

Figure A-26
Menu Bar Editor dialog box

Choose Activate a Feature, choose an item from the Feature Categories drop-down list and Features list box, and then add the feature to a menu by dragging it from the list box to the menu where you want it.

You can move a feature from one menu to another by dragging it; you can delete an item from a menu by dragging it off the menu; and you can add a dividing line to a menu by dragging the Separator icon to the menu where you want it. When you complete your Menu Bar layout, choose OK. Highlight the Menu Bar layout, and then choose Select and Close to use it in your document.

CUSTOMIZING MENU ITEMS

You can customize the text that appears on the menus and edit the Help prompts that accompany the menu items.

Choose File and Preferences, and then double-click on the Menu Bar icon. The Menu Bar Preferences dialog box will appear. Highlight the menu you want, and choose Edit. Note that you cannot edit the predefined menus. Double-click on the menu item you want to customize.

Key the text you want to appear on the menu in the Menu Item text box. Key an ampersand (&) in front of any character you want to become a mnemonic. Then key the text you want to appear as a description of the menu item in the Help Prompt text box.

Choose OK twice to save your changes.

To reset the menu to the default settings, press Ctrl+Alt+Shift+Backspace.

▶ STATUS BAR

At the bottom of the WordPerfect screen is the Status Bar. By default, it displays the current font on the far left, the Insert mode indication at left center, the position of the cursor in the document on the right, and the Select mode indicator in gray at right center. When you use the mouse to select text or choose Select from the Edit menu, Select will be displayed in black letters to tell you that WordPerfect is in Select mode. The default Status Bar also displays information about the status of features such as columns, macros, merges, paragraph style, and tables when appropriate. You can easily customize the Status Bar to notify you about other WordPerfect operating modes.

Choose File and Preferences, and then double-click on the Status Bar icon. The Status Bar Preferences dialog box will appear. (See Figure A-27.)

Figure A-27
Status Bar Preferences dialog box

CUSTOMIZING THE STATUS BAR

To add items to the Status Bar, you may need to first make room for them. As explained in the dialog box, you can delete an item by dragging it off the Status Bar; resize a box by dragging the left or right edge of the box; or change the order of an item by dragging it to a new position.

In the Status Bar Items list box is a checklist of features that can be included in the Status Bar. You can choose as many of these features as you want to add or remove from the status box by adding or removing the X in the adjacent check box. To change fonts for the Status Bar text and to customize the appearance of the Status Bar, choose Options. The Status Bar Options dialog box will appear, giving you font and size choices, as well as some appearance choices. (See Figure A-28.)

You can return to the original Status Bar by clicking on Default on the Status Bar Preferences dialog box.

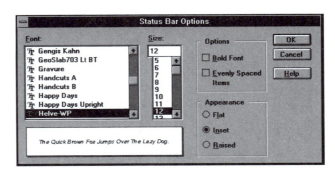

Figure A-28
Status Bar Options dialog box

APPENDIX A CUSTOMIZING OPTIONS

Appendix B
Guide to Troubleshooting with Reveal Codes

You will find Reveal Codes to be an invaluable feature to keep you informed about what is really happening in WordPerfect and to help you troubleshoot when you have problems. Whenever you have a problem, get in the habit of using Reveal Codes.

Whenever a document does not print as you intended, ask yourself the following questions:

1. Are the codes in the correct place? (before where the change is to take place)
2. Are there duplicate or extra codes in the document? Where are they located? Could they be causing problems?
3. Does the content to be affected show between paired codes?
4. Did I insert the proper code(s)?
5. Have I expanded the code and looked at all the information available to me?

The following list displays some of the WordPerfect 6.0 for Windows codes that may appear in your documents. You will see these codes when you use Reveal Codes. Some of these codes, known as expandable codes, show you additional information when the cursor is placed in front of the code or when you click on the code with the mouse pointer.

CODE	NAME OF CODE
[Bold]	Bold Text Attribute
[Bot Marg]	Bottom Margin
[Box]	Box
[Cell]	Table Cell
[Cntr Pgs]	Center Pages (Top to Bottom)
[Col Border]	Column Border
[Col Def]	Column Definition
[Date]	Date/Time Function
[Dbl Und]	Double Underline Text Attribute

CODE	NAME OF CODE
[Dec Tab]	Decimal–Aligned Tab
[Endnote]	Endnote
[Endnote Placement]	Endnote Placement
[Ext Large]	Extra Large Font Size
[Fine]	Fine Font Size
[Font]	Font
[Footer A]	Footer A
[Footer B]	Footer B
[Footnote]	Footnote
[Graph Line]	Graphics Line
[Hd Back Tab]	Hard Back Tab (Margin Release)
[Header A]	Header A
[Header B]	Header B
[Hd Flush Right]	Flush Right
[Hd Left Ind]	Indent
[HPg]	Hard Page Break
[HRt]	Hard Return
[Hyph]	Hyphenation State
[Italc]	Italic Text Attribute
[Just]	Justification
[Large]	Large Font Size
[Lft Mar]	Left Margin
[Left Tab]	Left–Aligned Tab
[Paper Sz/Typ]	Paper Size
[Para Border]	Paragraph Border
[Pg Border]	Page Border
[Pg Num Fmt]	Page Number Format
[Pg Num Pos]	Page Number Position

CODE	NAME OF CODE
[Right Tab]	Right–Aligned Tab
[Row]	Table Row
[Select]	Beginning of Selection
[Small]	Small Font Size
[SPg]	Soft Page Break
[SRt]	Soft Return
[Subscpt]	Subscript Text Position
[Suppress]	Suppress Header, Footer, Watermark, or Page Number
[Suprscpt]	Superscript Text Position
[Tab Set]	Tab Set
[Top Mar]	Top Margin
[Und]	Underline Text Attribute
[Very Large]	Very Large Font Size
[Wid/Orph]	Widow/Orphan Protect State

Index

A

Absolute tabs, *def.*, 44
All justification, *def.*, 49
Alphanumeric keys, *def.*, 196
Ascending keys, *def.*, 196
Associate, *def.*, 182
Auto wordwrap feature, *def.*, 14

B

Balanced Newspaper columns, *def.*, 165, 169–170
Block Protect, 104
Bold, italic, and underline, 68–69
Border/Fill button, 222
Borders, graphics, 199–203
Boxes, graphics, 220–223
Button Bar, *def.*, 2, 239–244
   tables, 154

C

Caption button, 220–221
Case, converting, 72–75
Cells
   floating, 161
   joining, 155
   selecting to be formatted or edited, 154
Center, 70–72
Center justification, *def.*, 48
Center tab, 42
Click, *def.*, 3
Clipboard, *def.*, 81
Close file, 18
   closing all, 143–144
Coach, 9
Code
   finding a word, phrase, or, 83–85
   replacing text and codes, 85–86

Codes, Reveal, 55–59
   expandable codes in, 103
   using for tables, 153
Columns
   column borders, 202–203
   newspaper, 165–170
   newspaper, *def.*, 165
   parallel, *def.*, 165, 170–172
Conditional End of Page, 104
Context-sensitive, *def.*, 9
Converting case, 72–75
Copy File, 143–144
Create Table, 151–153
Customizing graphics line, 204–207
Cut, Copy, and Paste commands, 81–82, 133

D

Data file merge, *def.*, 177, 178–182
Date, 13–15
Decimal tab, 42
Defaults, *def.*, 15
Delete File, 142–143
Deleting codes, 57
Descending keys, *def.*, 196
Dialog boxes, 6
   changing fonts through, 69
   for graphic lines, 205–206
   setting tabs through, 69
Directories, changing drives and, 139
Document assembly, *def.*, 99
Document Information, 122
Double-click, *def.*, 3
Double Indent, 46
Draft view, *def.*, 47
Drag, *def.*, 3
   drag and drop text, 83
   drag-and-release method, 4
Drives, changing directories and, 139

E

Editing text
   with keyboard, 27
   with mouse, 26
Endnotes and footnotes, 113–118
Envelopes, 62–64
   using Merge to print, 185–186
Expandable codes in Reveal Codes, 103
ExpressDocs templates, *def.*, 91

F

Feature Bar, *def.*, 105
Field, *def.*, 178
File, close, 18
Filename, 138
File Options, 140–145
Fill, *def.*, 199
Find and Replace, 83
Finding a word, phrase, or code, 83–85
Flush Right command, 72
Fonts, 67–69
Footers and headers, 105–108
Footnotes and endnotes, 113–118
Form file merge, *def.*, 177, 182–184
Full justification, *def.*, 48

G

Go To command, 108
Grammatik, 119–121
Graphics
   borders, 199–203
   boxes, editing, 220–223
   boxes in Reveal Codes, 209–210
   boxes, text boxes, 208–210

images, 218–225
lines, 203–207
Grayed, *def.*, 4
Gutter width, *def.*, 165

H

Hanging Indent, 46
Hard page breaks, 47–48, 116–118
Headers and footers, 105–108
　suppressing, 107–108
Help prompts, 10
Hyphenation, 87–88

I–J

Images
　graphics, 218–225
　TextArt, 215–218
Image Tools palette, 224
Indenting text, 45–47
Insert, 26–27
　current date, 13
　document file into an existing window, 100–101
Insertion Point, *def.*, 2
Italic, bold, and underline, 68–69
Justification
　centering with, 71
　changing, 48–49
　for tables, 155–157

K

Keyboard
　editing text with, 27
　using with menus, 5–6
　merge, 187–188
Keyed text
　centering, 71
　making font changes to, 70
Keys, sorting, 196
Keystrokes, using, 25–26

L

Label definitions, 191–194
Labels for mass mailings, 194–196
Left justification, *def.*, 48
Left tab, 42
Letters, using Merge to print, 185–186
Line Hyphenation, 87–88
Lines, graphics, 203–207
Line spacing, 15, 49–50
List Files of Type, 139
Logical page, *def.*, 192
Lowercase, converting, 72–75

M

Macros, 229–233
Margins
　changing, 40–41
　def., 15
　defining and changing Newspaper column, 166–167
Menu Bar, *def.*, 2, 246–247
Menus, using, 3–5
Merge
　data file, *def.*, 177, 178–182
　field, *def.*, 178
　form file, *def.*, 177, 182–184
　keyboard merge, 187–188
　merged document file, *def.*, 177, 185–188
　print data text files, 182
　print letters and envelopes, 185–186
　record, *def.*, 178
Mouse
　editing text with, 26
　using for graphics lines, 206
Moving through document, 24–26
Multi-page documents, 99–101

N–O

Newspaper columns, *def.*, 165
　Balanced, *def.*, 165
Number Type, 157–158
Numeric keys, *def.*, 196
Open File, 23–24, 138–140
　open more than one, 130
Orphans and widows, 103–104

P

Page, center, 72
Page borders, 201–202
Page breaks, 47–48
　using hard, 116–118
Page numbers, 101–103
　suppressing, 102–103
Page view, *def.*, 47
Palette, *def.*, 156
Paragraph borders, 200–201
Parallel columns, *def.*, 165, 170–172
Paste, Cut, and Copy commands, 81–82, 133
Physical page, *def.*, 192
Playing a macro, 230–231
Point, *def.*, 3
Point-and-click method, 4
Position button, 221
Power Bar, *def.*, 2, 17–18, 244–245
Preferences, 8
Print File, 141–142
Print File List, 144–145
Printing documents, 8, 17, 108–110
　letters and envelopes using merge, 185–186

Q

QuickCorrect, 61–62
QuickFinder, 145–147
QuickList, 147
QuickMenu, 4
QuickSelect, *def.*, 31

R

Record, *def.*, 178
Recording a macro, 229–230
Relative tabs, *def.*, 43
Release, *def.*, 3
Rename File, 143
Replace and Find, 83
Replacing text and codes, 85–86
Reveal Codes, 55–59
    expandable codes in, 103
    graphics boxes in, 209
    troubleshooting with, 57–59
    using in tables, 153
Right justification, *def.*, 48
Rotating images, 224–225
Rows, 159–160
Ruler Bar, 39–40
    changing margins, 40
    setting tabs through, 42–43
    using to set columns, 167–168

S

Save the document, 16–17
    with a different name, 28
Scroll Bar
    def., 2
    using, 24–25
Setting tabs, 41–45
Shading/line styles, 156–157
Size of the Reveal Codes screen, adjusting, 57
Sorting, 196
Spacing, changing line, 49–50
Spelling, checking, 59–61
Spreadsheets, 161
Standard templates, *def.*, 91
Status Bar, *def.*, 2, 153, 167, 248
Storing data, 8
Suppressing
    header or footer, 107–108
    page number, 102–103
Switching between documents, 132–133
System requirements, 8

T

Tables
    adding and deleting text and calculating totals, 158–160
    Button Bar, 154
    changing column widths, 157
    changing justification, 157
    creating, 151–153
    deleting, 159
    editing structure, 153–158
    shading/line styles, 156–157
Tabs, 15, 41–45
    tab settings in columns, 169
Template, *def.*, 91, 92–95
TextArt images, 215–218
Text blocks, selecting, 29–31
Text boxes, 208–210
Thesaurus, 118–119
Title Bar, *def.*, 1
Two-Page view, *def.*, 47
Typeover, 27

U

Undelete command, 32–34
Underline, bold, and italic, 68–69
Undo command, 32
Uppercase, converting, 72–75

V

View pull-down menu, 47
Viewing a file, 140
Viewing multiple windows, 131–132

W

Watermark, 232–233
Widows and orphans, 103–104
Windows
    closing document, 133–134
    exit, 19
    viewing multiple, 131–132
WordPerfect 6.0 for DOS, 10
WordPerfect 6.0 for Windows
    conventions, 7
    exit, 18
    starting, 1
    using, 2–3
WordPerfect macros, 232–233
Wrap Text, 223

Z

Zoom, 28–29